# Making Words
# First Grade

## 100 Hands-On Lessons for
## Phonemic Awareness, Phonics, and Spelling

**Patricia M. Cunningham**

*Wake Forest University*

**Dorothy P. Hall**

*Wake Forest University*

Boston • New York • San Francisco
Mexico City • Montreal • Toronto • London • Madrid • Munich • Paris
Hong Kong • Singapore • Tokyo • Cape Town • Sydney

**Executive Editor:**   Aurora Martínez Ramos
**Series Editorial Assistant:**   Kara Kikel
**Director of Professional Development:**   Alison Maloney
**Marketing Manager:**   Danae April
**Production Editor:**   Annette Joseph
**Editorial Production Service:**   Lynda Griffiths
**Composition Buyer:**   Linda Cox
**Manufacturing Buyer:**   Linda Morris
**Electronic Composition:**   Denise Hoffman
**Interior Design:**   Denise Hoffman
**Cover Administrator:**   Kristina Mose-Libon

For related titles and support materials, visit our online catalog at www.ablongman.com.

Between the time website information is gathered and then published, it is not unusual for some sites to have closed. Also, the transcription of URLs can result in typographical errors. The publisher would appreciate notification where these errors occur so that they may be corrected in subsequent editions.

ISBN-10: 0-205-58095-5
ISBN-13: 978-0-205-58095-8

Printed in the United States of America

10  9  8  7  6          11

**Photos:** Dorothy P. Hall.

*Pat*                    *Dottie*

## Patricia M. Cunningham

From the day I entered first grade, I knew I wanted to be a first-grade teacher. In 1965, I graduated from the University of Rhode Island and began my teaching career teaching first grade in Key West, Florida. For the next several years, I taught a variety of grades and worked as a curriculum coordinator and special reading teacher in Florida and Indiana. From the very beginning, I worried about the children who struggled in learning to read and so I devised a variety of alternative strategies to teach them to read. In 1974, I received my Ph.D. in Reading Education from the University of Georgia.

I developed the Making Words activity while working with Title I teachers in North Carolina, where I was the Director of Reading for Alamance County Schools. I have been the Director of Elementary Education at Wake Forest University in Winston-Salem, North Carolina, since 1980 and have worked with numerous teachers to develop hands-on, engaging ways to teach phonics and spelling. In 1991, I wrote *Phonics They Use: Words for Reading and Writing*, which is currently available in its fourth edition. Along with Richard Allington, I also wrote *Classrooms that Work* and *Schools that Work*.

Dottie Hall and I have worked together on many projects. In 1989, we began developing the Four Blocks Framework, a comprehensive approach to literacy that is used in many schools in the United States and Canada. Dottie and I have produced many books together, including the first *Making Words* books and the *Month by Month Phonics* books. These *Making Words* for grade levels kindergarten to fifth grade are in response to requests by teachers across the years to have Making Words lessons with a scope and sequence tailored to their various grade levels. We hope you and your students will enjoy these Making Words lessons and we would love to hear your comments and suggestions.

# Dorothy P. Hall

I always wanted to teach young children. After graduating from Worcester State College in Massachusetts, I taught first and second grades. Two years later, I moved to North Carolina, where I continued teaching in the primary grades. Many children I worked with in the newly integrated schools struggled in learning to read. Wanting to increase my knowledge, I received my M.Ed. and Ed.D. in Reading from the University of North Carolina at Greensboro. I also worked at Wake Forest University, where I met and began to work with Pat Cunningham.

After three years of teaching at the college level I returned to the public schools and taught third and fourth grades and served as a reading and curriculum coordinator for my school district. At this time Pat Cunningham and I began to collaborate on a number of projects. In 1989, we developed the Four Blocks Framework, a comprehensive approach to literacy in grades 1, 2, and 3, which we called Big Blocks. Later, we expanded the program to include kindergarten, calling it Building Blocks. By 1999, Pat and I had written four *Making Words* books, a series of *Month by Month Phonics* books, and *The Teacher's Guide to Four Blocks*, and I retired from the school system to devote more time to consulting and writing. I also went back to work at Wake Forest University, where I taught courses in reading, children's literature, and language arts instruction for elementary education students.

Today, I am Director of the Four Blocks Center at Wake Forest University and enjoy working with teachers and administrators around the country presenting workshops on Four Blocks, Building Blocks, guided reading strategies, and phonics instruction. I have also written several books with teachers. One request Pat and I have had for a number of years is to revise the *Making Words* by grade level and include a scope and sequence for the phonics instruction taught. Here it is—Enjoy!

# Contents

# Introduction

Many teachers first discovered Making Words in the first edition of *Phonics They Use*, which was published in 1991. Since then, teachers around the world have used Making Words lessons to help children discover how our spelling system works. Making Words lessons are an example of a type of instruction called guided discovery. In order to truly learn and retain strategies, children must discover them. But many children do not make discoveries about words on their own. In Making Words lessons, children are guided to make those discoveries.

Making Words is a popular activity with both teachers and children. Children love manipulating letters to make words and figuring out the secret word that can be made with all the letters. While children are having fun making words, they are also learning important information about phonics and spelling. As children manipulate the letters to make the words, they learn how small changes, such as changing just one letter or moving the letters around, result in completely new words. Children develop phonemic awareness as they stretch out words and listen for the sounds they hear and the order of those sounds.

## Teaching a Making Words Lesson

Every Making Words lesson has three parts. First, children manipulate the letters to *make* words. This part of the lesson uses a spelling approach to help children learn letter sounds and how to segment words and blend letters. In the second part of the lesson, children sort words according to patterns. Early in first grade, the patterns we sort for are beginning letters. In later lessons, children learn to *sort* words into rhymes. We end each lesson by helping children *transfer* what they have learned to reading and spelling new words. In the first 30 lessons, we focus on transferring beginning letter-sound knowledge. In later lessons, children learn how the rhyming words they sorted help them read and spell lots of other rhyming words.

Each Making Words lesson begins with short easy words and moves to longer, more complex words. The last word is always the secret word—a word that can be made with all the letters. As children arrange the letters, a child who has successfully made a word goes to the pocket chart and makes the word with big letters. Children who don't have the word made correctly quickly fix their word so that they're ready for the next word. The small changes between most words encourage even those children who have not made a word perfectly to fix it because they soon realize that having the current word correctly spelled increases their chances of spelling the next word correctly. In first grade, each lesson includes 8 to 12 words, including the secret word that can be made with all the letters.

In Part Two of a Making Words lesson, children sort the words into patterns. Many children discover patterns just through making the words in the carefully sequenced order, but some children need more explicit guidance. This guidance happens when all the words have been made and the teacher guides the children to sort them into patterns. They also sort the words according to their first letter and learn that words that begin with the same letter begin with the same sound. Children sort the words into rhyming words and notice that words that rhyme have the same spelling pattern.

Many children know letter sounds and patterns but do not apply these to decode an unknown word encountered during reading or to spell a word they need while writing. This is the reason that every Making Words lesson ends with a transfer step. After words are sorted according to beginning letters, children apply these beginning letter sounds to new words. When words are sorted according to rhyme, children use these rhyming words to decode and spell new words. Here is an example of how you might conduct a Making Words lesson and cue the children to the changes and words you want them to make. (This lesson is #56 in *Making Words First Grade*.)

# Beginning the Lesson

The children all have the letters:  **a  e  g  m  n  s  t**

These same letters—big enough for all to see—are displayed in a pocket chart. The letter cards have lowercase letters on one side and capital letters on the other side. The vowels are in a different color.

The words the children are going to make are written on index cards. These words will be placed in the pocket chart as the words are made and will be used for the Sort and Transfer steps of the lesson.

The teacher begins the lesson by having the children hold up and name each letter as the teacher holds up the big letters in the pocket chart.

> "Hold up and name each letter as I hold up the big letter. Let's start with your vowels. Show me your **a** and your **e**. Now show me your **g**, **m**, **n**, **s**, and **t**. Today you have 7 letters. In a few minutes, we will see if anyone can figure out the secret word that uses all 7 letters."

## Part One: Making Words

> "Use 3 letters to spell the word **eat**. We **eat** at 11:25."

(Find someone with **eat** spelled correctly and send that child to spell **eat** with the big letters.)

> "Use 3 letters to spell **net**. In tennis, you try to hit the ball over the **net**."
>
> "Change the first letter in **net** to spell **met**. I **met** my cousin at the mall."
>
> "Change the first letter again to spell **set**. It is my job to **set** the table."
>
> "Add a letter you can't hear to **set** to spell **seat**. Please stay in your **seat**."

(Quickly send someone with the correct spelling to the big letters. Keep the pace brisk. Do not wait until everyone has **seat** spelled with their little letters. It is fine if some children are making **seat** as **seat** is being spelled with the big letters.)

"Change the first letter in **seat** to spell **neat**. On Fridays, we leave our classroom clean and **neat**."

"Change the first letter again to spell **meat**. Vegetarians don't eat **meat**."

"Use the same letters in **meat** but move them around so they spell **team**. What is your favorite football **team**?"

"Use 4 letters to spell **east**. The sun rises in the **east**."

"Clear your holders and start over to spell another 4 letter word: **stem**. Most plants have a root, leaves, and a **stem**."

"Use a letter you can't hear to turn **stem** into **steam**. When you heat water, it turns into **steam**."

"I have just one word left. It is the secret word you can make with all your letters. See if you can figure it out."

(Give the children one minute to figure out the secret word. Then give clues if needed.) Let someone who figures it out go to the big letters and spell the secret word: **magnets**.

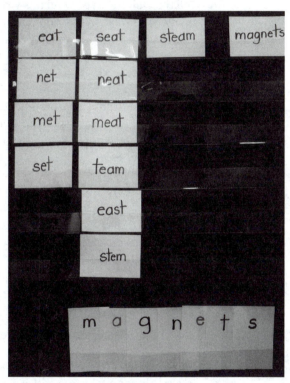

## Part Two: Sorting the Words into Patterns

Using the index cards with words you made, place them in the pocket chart as the children pronounce and chorally spell each. Give them a quick reminder of how they made these words:

"First we spelled a 3 letter word, **eat, e-a-t**."

"We spelled another 3 letter word, **net, n-e-t**."

"We changed the first letter to spell **met, m-e-t**."

"We changed the first letter again to spell **set, s-e-t**."

"We added the **a** you don't hear to change set to **seat, s-e-a-t**."

"We changed the first letter to spell **neat, n-e-a-t**."

"We changed the first letter again to spell **meat, m-e-a-t**."

"We used 4 letters to spell **east, e-a-s-t**."

"We spelled one more 4 letter word, **stem, s-t-e-m**."

"We added the silent **a** to change stem to **steam, s-t-e-a-m**."

"Finally, we spelled the secret word using all our letters, **magnets, m-a-g-n-e-t-s**."

Next have the children sort the rhyming words. Take one of each set of rhyming words and place them in the pocket chart.

**net**        **seat**        **team**

Ask three children to find the other words that rhyme and place them under the ones you pulled out.

| eat | team | net |
|-----|------|-----|
| seat | steam | met |
| neat | | set |
| meat | | |

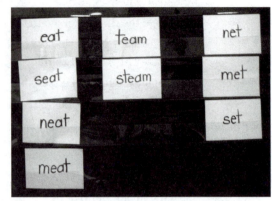

Have the children chorally pronounce the sets of rhyming words.

## Part Three: Transfer

Tell the children to pretend it is writing time and they need to spell some words that rhyme with some of the words they made today. Have the children use whiteboards or half-sheets of paper to write the words. Say sentences that children might want to write that include a rhyming word. Work together to decide which words the target word rhymes with and to decide how to spell it.

"Boys and girls, let's pretend it is writing time. Terry is writing about going fishing and he is trying to spell the word **stream**. Let's all say **stream** and stretch out the beginning letters. What 3 letters do you hear at the beginning of **stream**?"

Have the children stretch out **stream** and listen for the beginning letters. When they tell you that **stream** begins with **str**, write **str** on an index card and have the children write **str** on their papers or whiteboards.

Take the index card with **str** on it to the pocket chart and hold it under each column of words as you lead the children to chorally pronounce the words and decide if **stream** rhymes with them:

"Net, met, set, stream." Children should show you "thumbs down."

"Seat, neat, meat, eat, stream." Children should again show you "thumbs down."

"Team, steam, stream." Children should show you "thumbs up."

Finish writing **stream** on your index card by adding **eam** to **str** and place **stream** in the pocket chart under **team** and **steam**. Have the children write **eam** next to **str**.

"Now let's pretend Carla is writing and telling you that she and her family went out for ice cream last night as a special **treat**. Carla is trying to spell **treat**. Let's stretch out **treat** and listen for the two letters we hear at the beginning of **treat**."

Write **tr** on the index card and have the students write **tr**.

Take the index card to the pocket chart and hold it under each column of words as you lead the children to chorally pronounce the words and decide if **treat** rhymes with them:

"Net, met, set, treat." Children should show you "thumbs down."

"Seat, neat, meat, eat, treat." Children should show you "thumbs up."

Finish writing **treat** on your index card by adding **eat** to **tr** and place **treat** in the pocket chart under **seat**, **neat**, **meat**, and **eat**. Have the children write **eat** next to **tr** to complete their word.

Follow the same procedure to lead the children to use the rhyming word to spell **wet**.

We hope this sample lesson has helped you see how a Making Words lesson works and how Making Words lessons help children develop phonemic awareness, phonics, and spelling skills. Most important, we hope you see that in every lesson children will practice applying the patterns they are learning to reading and spelling new words.

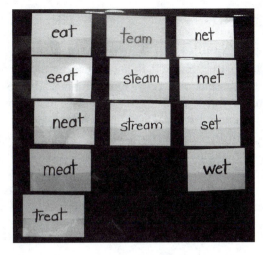

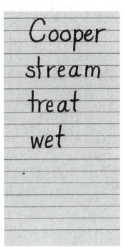

# Scope and Sequence for Making Words First Grade Lessons

*Making Words First Grade* contains 100 lessons that teach all the phonics, spelling, and phonemic awareness skills included in most first-grade curriculums. The lessons lead children through a systematic and sequential phonics curriculum. All lessons include practice with the phonemic awareness skills of segmenting and blending as children stretch out words they are making and blend the letters to make new words. Because teaching children letter-sound relationships is easier than teaching children to actually use these letter-sound relationships, all lessons include a transfer step in which children apply the sounds they are learning to spelling new words.

The first 20 lessons teach the common sounds for the vowels and most useful consonants. Lessons 21 to 30 review the vowel sounds and teach the sounds for *k, sh, ch, th,* and *ck.* In lessons 31 to 40, children manipulate two vowels to spell words and learn the sounds for *j* and *w.* The *r* controlled vowels are introduced and practiced in lessons 51 to 60. The remaining lessons review all the vowel and consonant sounds taught and introduce the consonants *v, x, y,* and *z* and the vowel combinations, *ee, ea, oa, ay, ai, a-e, ue, i-e, igh, a-e, o-e, oo, ow, ou, oy,* and *aw.* After the letter sounds are taught, they continue to be practiced and reviewed in the lessons that follow.

| Lessons | Vowels Taught | Consonants |
|---|---|---|
| Lessons 1–10 | *a* | *b c d f g h l m n p r s t* |
| Lessons 11–20 | *e i o u* | |
| Lessons 21–30 | | *k ch sh th ck* |
| Lessons 31–40 | 2 vowels | *j w* |
| Lessons 41–50 | *ar ir or ur* | *v* |
| Lessons 51–60 | *er ee ea oa* | *x* |
| Lessons 61–70 | *ay ai ue y* | *y* |
| Lessons 71–80 | *i-e igh a-e* | *z* |
| Lessons 81–90 | *o-e* | |
| Lessons 91–100 | *oo ow ou oy aw* | |

# Assessment

After every 10 lessons, there is an assessment you can use to determine how individual children are growing in their phonics, phonemic awareness, and spelling skills. The first four assessments measure children's letter name and sound knowledge and their ability to blend and segment words. These are individual assessments but should only take a few minutes for each child. It is not necessary to do these assessments with any child who you are *sure* has the skills. The last six assessments can be done with your whole class of children but you need to be sure that each child is writing the words without being able to see what anyone else is writing. Record sheets are included to help you monitor each child's progress. In addition to assessing for the new skills taught, you may want to recheck children on items they were not successful at in previous assessments. Reproducible record sheets are included in the back of this book.

# Organizing to Teach Making Words

The materials you need to teach a Making Words lesson are quite simple. You need a pocket chart in which to display the word correctly made with the pocket chart letters. You need a set of pocket chart letters big enough for all the children to see. Also, you need index cards on which to write the words children will make and the transfer words. Most teachers store their index cards for each lesson in an envelope.

The children need small letter cards and a holder in which to make the words. The letter holder is easily made from half a file folder. The holder is very important to the success of your lesson because it focuses all the children on making their own words. Without the holders, children who are not very fast at making words will simply look at

## How to Make a Letter Holder

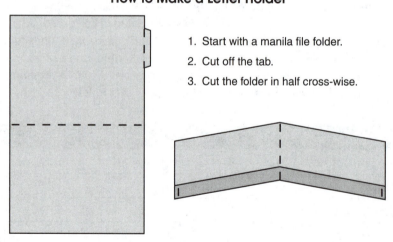

1. Start with a manila file folder.
2. Cut off the tab.
3. Cut the folder in half cross-wise.

Prepare each half of the folder as follows:

4. Fold up one inch on the bottom edge to form a shallow pocket.
5. Press firmly along folded edge with a ruler to flatten.
6. Staple side edges.

You now have a letter holder that your students can set on their desks to put letters in when making words.

the letters of a quick child seated near them and put down the same letters. The learning in a Making Words lesson does not occur when the child moves the letters. Rather, the learning happens when the child says the word and thinks about where to move the letters. Making Words is a guided discovery activity and you want all your children to engage in the discovery. As the children are making words, walk behind them and select a child with the word made correctly to make the words with the pocket chart letters. Choose your struggling readers to go to the pocket chart and make some of the easier words and they will stay engaged with the lesson because they are experiencing some success. Be sure to ask all children to fix their word if it was not correct when the word is made in the pocket chart.

Another advantage of using the holder is that it allows you to get all the letters quickly out of the hands of the children before the sorting step of the lesson. Have all the children make the secret word in their holder once it is made in the pocket chart. Let them hold up their holders to show you the secret word and then have them close their holders with all the letters in them. They will pay better attention to the sorting activity if they do not still have the letters in front of them to distract them.

A final reason to use the holders is that they are the most efficient way to distribute the letters the children need. When you are going to do a Making Words lesson, put the holders and letters on a table and have the children walk by and pick up a holder and one letter from each container. We call this "stuffing your holder." When the lesson ends, collect everyone's holder with the letters still in there. At the end of the day, appoint some "holder unstuffer helpers" to take the letters out of the holders and place them on the appropriate container. Place the letters into the appropriate zippered bag and you have put everything away—neat and tidy and ready for the next lesson.

At the back of this book, you will find reproducible letters. Copy these on card stock and cut them with your paper cutter. Use a different color paper for the vowels and a third color for *y*, which is sometimes a vowel and sometimes a consonant. Make twice as many letters as you have children because some words need two of the same letter.

## Making Words Homework

Because children like manipulating the letters and coming up with more words than we have time to make in the lesson, a Making Words Take-Home Sheet is a popular activity. You will find a duplicatable template in the back of this book. Write the letters in the boxes at the top in alphabetical order with vowels and then consonants. Before leaving the classroom, have the children turn the sheet over and write the capital letters on the back. When they get home, the children cut or tear the letters from the top and then fill the boxes with words. They can use words made in class or other words. Children enjoy this homework assignment because they know the secret word and they love watching parents and others try to figure it out!

# Making Words Lessons Are Multilevel

Making Words lessons are designed so that all your students, regardless of level, will feel challenged and will experience success. In the example lesson described here, the focus was on the **ea** pattern. Children spelled five words—**seat**, **neat**, **meat**, **east**, and **steam**—in which they could only hear the **e** but they needed the **ea** to spell the word. Twice in the lesson, they made a word and then added the **a** to change the word. They added the **a** to change **set** to **seat** and **stem** to **steam**. The lesson, however, included some easier words that reviewed the sound of **e** taught much earlier. Students manipulated letters to spell **net**, **met**, **set**, and **stem**. The inclusion of a secret word—a word that can be made with all the letters—provides a challenge for your most able spellers. From the time they get the letters, they are manipulating them in their minds to try to figure out what word can be spelled with all the letters. Most of your children will not figure out that **a**, **e**, **g**, **m**, **n**, **s**, and **t** can be put together to spell **magnets**, but including a secret word in every lesson makes the lesson multilevel for even your quickest word wizards!

Another way in which Making Words lessons are multilevel involves the three parts of the lesson. We ask children to say each word before they make it and encourage them to stretch out words. This saying and stretching provides crucial practice for children who still need to work on the phonemic awareness skill of segmenting. In the sort segment of the lesson, before we sort the words, we place them in the pocket chart and have the children read the words. As they read the words, children practice the phonemic awareness skill of blending. Sorting the words into beginning letter patterns and rhyming patterns helps children learn the sounds for beginning letters and vowel patterns. Finally, we include a transfer step in every lesson. Children stretch out the transfer word to determine the beginning letters and then use the rhyming words made to spell new words. Every Making Words lesson provides multiple opportunities for children to develop phonemic awareness, learn phonics patterns, and transfer their knowledge to spelling new words. For many years, teachers have enjoyed doing Making Words lessons with their entire class of students, confident in the knowledge that all children, regardless of level, will grow in their phonics, phonemic awareness, and spelling skills as they participate in these active hands-on learning lessons. We hope you and your first-graders enjoy these lessons created just for you and them! (For other phonics lessons tailor made for first-graders, see *Month by Month Phonics for First Grade*, by Patricia M. Cunningham and Dorothy P. Hall, published by Carson-Dellosa in 2003.)

# Lessons 1-10

The first ten lessons teach the sounds for the most common consonants by having children make words that only use the vowel **a**. The goal for these beginning lessons is that children learn to segment words and blend sounds, the sounds for **a** and the common consonants, and to transfer the letter sounds they are learning to begin to spell words.

# Lesson 1

## stand

**Letters:**  **a, d, n, s, t**   (The consonants **s**, **t**, **n**, **d** and the vowel **a** are introduced.)

**Words to Make:**  at   an   and   ant   tan   sat   sad   sand   stand

## Part One • Making Words

Have the children arrange their letters in front of their holders to match the pocket chart letters, with the vowel first and the other letters in alphabetical order.

Begin the lesson by naming each pocket-chart letter. Ask the children to hold up their little letter cards as you hold up the large letter cards. Have them show both lowercase and capital letters. Explain that the **a** is on a different color because it is a vowel and that every word needs at least one vowel. Explain that the capital letter is used to spell names, and have the children notice that their own names all begin with capital letters. Tell the students that they won't be making any names in these first lessons so they will use only the lowercase letters. Later, when they are experienced at making words, the lessons will include some names.

> **at**  "The first word we are going to spell is **at**. We are **at** school. Everyone say **at**. Use 2 letters to spell **at**."

Look in the students' holders and choose a child who has **at** spelled correctly to spell **at** with the pocket-chart letters. Have the children chorally spell **at** after **at** is made with the pocket-chart letters and fix their word if it is not correct. Next, remove the **t** in **at** and ask the children to remove the **t** from their holders.

> **an**  "The next word we are going to spell is **an**. I brought **an** apple for snack. Everyone say **an**."

Look in the students' holders and choose a child who has **an** spelled correctly to spell **an** with the pocket-chart letters. Have the children chorally spell **an** after **an** is made.

**and**      "Keep **a-n** in your holders and add a letter to the end to spell **and**. I like peanut butter **and** jelly. Everyone say **and**."

Continue the lesson, giving children explicit instruction about which letters to remove and where to add letters. Put each word in a sentence and have children say each word before making it. Have them "stretch" words to provide practice for children who are still learning to segment words. Let a child who has spelled the word correctly come to the front of the room and make that word with the pocket-chart letters. Choose your struggling readers when the word is an easy word and choose your advanced readers for harder words. Have the children chorally spell each word after it is made in the pocket chart and fix their word to match.

**ant**      "Remove the **d** and add a different letter to the end to spell **ant**. A tiny **ant** crawled on my desk. Everyone say **ant**. Add a letter to **a-n** to spell **ant**."

**tan**      "Don't take any letters out. Move the letters in **ant** to spell **tan**. I saw a **tan** SUV. Everyone say **tan**. Listen for where you hear the letters to decide where to move them to spell **tan**."

**sat**      "Take all your letters out of your holder. Use three letters to spell **sat**. I **sat** with my friends at lunch. Everyone say **sat**. Stretch the word **sat** and listen for where you hear the letters."

**sad**      "Remove the **t** and add a different letter to spell **sad**. I was **sad** when my dog died. Everyone say **sad**."

**sand**      "Move your **d** away from the **a** to make some space to add a letter. Add one letter to spell **sand**. Do you like to dig in the **sand**? Everyone say **sand**."

**stand**      "We have one more word to spell. Add the **t** someplace in **sand** to spell **stand**. We **stand** up when we say the Pledge of Allegiance. Everyone say **sand**. Stretch the word **stand** and listen to where you hear the **t**."

End the making words part of the lesson by having one child spell **stand** with the pocket-chart letters and letting everyone hold up their holders to show you **stand** made in their holders. Have them close the holders and turn their attention to the pocket chart.

## Part Two • Sorting Words (Sort for beginnings sounds **a**, **t**, and **s**.)

Tell your students that they are going to say all the words they spelled and then sort them according to the first letter. Using the index cards with the words, place them in the pocket chart and have the children pronounce them. Remind the children of what they changed to make each word as you put each word in the pocket chart.

"First we used 2 letters to spell **at**, **a-t**."

"We changed the **t** to an **n** to spell **an**, **a-n**."

"We added the **d** to spell **and**, **a-n-d**."

"We changed the **d** to a **t** to spell **ant**, **a-n-t**."

"We moved the letters in **ant** around to spell **tan**, **t-a-n**."

"We cleared our holders and started again to spell **sat**, **s-a-t**."

"We changed the **t** to a **d** to spell **sad**, **s-a-d**."

"We added the **n** before the **d** to spell **sand**, **s-a-n-d**."

"We added the **t** after the **s** to change sand into **stand**, **s-t-a-n-d**."

Choose three children to come to the front of the room and sort the words according to the first letter. One child should find all the **a** words, another child all the **t** words, and another child all the **s** words.

| at | tan | sand |
|----|-----|------|
| an | | sat |
| and | | sad |
| ant | | stand |

# Part Three • Transfer (Find words in the room that begin with the letters **s**, **t**, **a**, **n**, and **d**.)

The final step will take only a few minutes but is crucial if children are going to use the letter-sound relationships they are learning in the Making Words lessons. The focus of these earlier lessons is on learning consonant sounds, and thus the transfer step asks students to think about what letter some common words begin with.

Ask the children to open their letter holders and take out the letters and lay them down in front of their holders in the same order they had at the beginning of the lesson. Order the pocket-chart letters in the same way.

Say some words and have the children repeat the words and then hold up the letter they think that word begins with. Appoint a pocket-chart helper to hold up the same letter after the children have held up their small letters. If some children are holding up the wrong letter, have them pronounce the word again and hold up the letter being held up by the pocket-chart holder.

Because children are concrete learners and because they can forget what word they are supposed to be working on, use real objects and pictures to help them stay focused on the word. (In these first lessons, try to use words with just one beginning sound. Avoid words that begin with blends, such as *students*.)

For this lesson, use things in your classroom that begin with **a**, **d**, **n**, **s**, and **t**. Have your students point to the object as they say the word before showing the letter that word begins with. Here are some possible words. You may find better ones in looking around your classroom.

**alphabet   door   teacher   noses   desks   sink   scissors   notebooks   teeth**

# Lesson 2
## hands

Letters:  a   d   h   n   s   (The letter **h** is introduced.)

**Make:**   as   an   and   has   had   sad   sand   hand   hands

**Sort:**

| as | has | sad |
|----|-----|------|
| an | had | sand |
| and | hand | |
| | hands | |

**Transfer:**   (Point to objects in the room that begin with today's letters.)

| alphabet | door | hair |
|----------|------|------|
| noses | desks | scissors |
| hands | sink | notebooks |

## Make Words

- Have children name and hold up letters.
- Tell children how many letters to use to make each word.
- Have children say each word and stretch out some words.
- Give sentences to clarify meaning.
- Give specific instructions on how to change words:
  — Add one letter.
  — Change the first letter.
  — Use the same letters.
- Have children clear their holders before making an unrelated word.
- Have children correct their word once it is made in the pocket chart.

## Sort Words

- Put words in pocket chart in the order made.
- Have children say and spell each word.
- Remind them of how each word was changed to spell the new word.
- Select one word beginning with each letter and line up in columns.
- Let children choose the other words that begin that way.
- Have children pronounce the words.

## Transfer Words

- Have children take their letters out of their holders.
- Point to some objects in the room that begin with these letters.
- Have children say the word and hold up the beginning letter.

# Lesson 3

## bands

**Letters:** a  b  d  n  s   (The letter **b** is introduced.)

Children have already made many of these words and should make them relatively quickly.

 **Make:**   as   an   ban   bad   and   sad   sand   band   bands

 **Sort:**

| as | ban | sad |
|----|-----|-----|
| an | bad | sand |
| and | band | |
| | bands | |

**Transfer:**   (Point to objects in the room that begin with today's letters.)

| alphabet | door | books |
|----------|------|-------|
| noses | desks | board |
| boys | sink | notebooks |

## Make Words

- Have children name and hold up letters.
- Tell children how many letters to use to make each word.
- Have children say each word and stretch out some words.
- Give sentences to clarify meaning.
- Give specific instructions on how to change words:
    — Add one letter.
    — Change the first letter.
    — Use the same letters.
- Have children clear their holders before making an unrelated word.
- Have children correct their word once it is made in the pocket chart.

## Sort Words

- Put words in pocket chart in the order made.
- Have children say and spell each word.
- Remind them of how each word was changed to spell the new word.
- Select one word beginning with each letter and line up in columns.
- Let children choose the other words that begin that way.
- Have children pronounce the words.

## Transfer Words

- Have children take their letters out of their holders.
- Point to some objects in the room that begin with these letters.
- Have children say the word and hold up the beginning letter.

# Lesson 4

## blast

**Letters:** [a] [b] [l] [s] [t]   (The letter **l** is introduced.)

Children have already made many of these words and should make them relatively quickly. Pictures of food are needed for the transfer activity.

**Make:**   as   at   sat   bat   tab   lab   bats   stab   last   blast

**Sort:**

| | | | | |
|---|---|---|---|---|
| as | bat | sat | last | tab |
| at | bats | stab | lab | |
| | blast | | | |

**Transfer:**   (Show pictures or name foods that begin with today's letters.)

| | | |
|---|---|---|
| apples | bananas | soup |
| lemons | lollipops | biscuits |
| sandwich | beans | lettuce |

## Make Words

- Have children name and hold up letters.
- Tell children how many letters to use to make each word.
- Have children say each word and stretch out some words.
- Give sentences to clarify meaning.
- Give specific instructions on how to change words:
  — Add one letter.
  — Change the first letter.
  — Use the same letters.
- Have children clear their holders before making an unrelated word.
- Have children correct their word once it is made in the pocket chart.

## Sort Words

- Put words in pocket chart in the order made.
- Have children say and spell each word.
- Remind them of how each word was changed to spell the new word.
- Select one word beginning with each letter and line up in columns.
- Let children choose the other words that begin that way.
- Have children pronounce the words.

## Transfer Words

- Have children take their letters out of their holders.
- Point to some objects in the room that begin with these letters.
- Have children say the word and hold up the beginning letter.

# Lesson 5
## brand

**Letters:** [a] [b] [d] [n] [r]   (The letter **r** is introduced.)

You will need some pictures of food that begin with **r** for the transfer activity.

**Make:**   an   ad   and   ran   ban   bad   band   brand

**Sort:**

| an | ban | ran |
|----|-----|-----|
| ad | bad | |
| and | band | |
| | brand | |

**Transfer:**   (Show pictures or name foods that begin with today's letters.)

| apples | bananas | rice |
|--------|---------|------|
| biscuits | radishes | beans |
| ravioli | beans | raisins |

## Make Words

- Have children name and hold up letters.
- Tell children how many letters to use to make each word.
- Have children say each word and stretch out some words.
- Give sentences to clarify meaning.
- Give specific instructions on how to change words:
  — Add one letter.
  — Change the first letter.
  — Use the same letters.
- Have children clear their holders before making an unrelated word.
- Have children correct their word once it is made in the pocket chart.

## Sort Words

- Put words in pocket chart in the order made.
- Have children say and spell each word.
- Remind them of how each word was changed to spell the new word.
- Select one word beginning with each letter and line up in columns.
- Let children choose the other words that begin that way.
- Have children pronounce the words.

## Transfer Words

- Have children take their letters out of their holders.
- Point to some objects in the room that begin with these letters.
- Have children say the word and hold up the beginning letter.

# Lesson 6
## grand

**Letters:** a d n g r (The letter **g** is introduced.)

Collect some pictures of animals that begin with these letters for the transfer activity.

**Make:** ad an and ran rag drag grad grand

**Sort:**

| an | grad | ran | drag |
|----|------|-----|------|
| ad | grand | rag | |
| and | | | |

**Transfer:** (Show pictures or name animals that begin with today's letters.)

| dog | duck | ants |
|-----|------|------|
| goat | alligator | gorilla |
| rabbit | raccoon | goldfish |

## Make Words

- Have children name and hold up letters.
- Tell children how many letters to use to make each word.
- Have children say each word and stretch out some words.
- Give sentences to clarify meaning.
- Give specific instructions on how to change words:
  — Add one letter.
  — Change the first letter.
  — Use the same letters.
- Have children clear their holders before making an unrelated word.
- Have children correct their word once it is made in the pocket chart.

## Sort Words

- Put words in pocket chart in the order made.
- Have children say and spell each word.
- Remind them of how each word was changed to spell the new word.
- Select one word beginning with each letter and line up in columns.
- Let children choose the other words that begin that way.
- Have children pronounce the words.

## Transfer Words

- Have children take their letters out of their holders.
- Point to some objects in the room that begin with these letters.
- Have children say the word and hold up the beginning letter.

## strap

**Letters:** | a | p | r | s | t | (The letter **p** is introduced.)

Collect some pictures of animals that begin with **p**, **s**, and **t** for the transfer activity.

**Make:**  as   at   rat   pat   sat   sap   rap   tap   trap   traps   strap

**Sort:**

| as | rat | sat | trap | pat |
|------|------|-------|-------|------|
| at | rap | strap | traps | |
| | | sap | tap | |

**Transfer:**   (Show pictures or name animals that begin with today's letters.)

| turtle | panda | rabbit | seal |
|--------|-------|--------|------|
| tiger | alligator | ant | |
| turkey | raccoon | pig | |

# Make Words

- Have children name and hold up letters.
- Tell children how many letters to use to make each word.
- Have children say each word and stretch out some words.
- Give sentences to clarify meaning.
- Give specific instructions on how to change words:
  — Add one letter.
  — Change the first letter.
  — Use the same letters.
- Have children clear their holders before making an unrelated word.
- Have children correct their word once it is made in the pocket chart.

# Sort Words

- Put words in pocket chart in the order made.
- Have children say and spell each word.
- Remind them of how each word was changed to spell the new word.
- Select one word beginning with each letter and line up in columns.
- Let children choose the other words that begin that way.
- Have children pronounce the words.

# Transfer Words

- Have children take their letters out of their holders.
- Point to some objects in the room that begin with these letters.
- Have children say the word and hold up the beginning letter.

# Lesson 8

## claps

**Letters:** | a | c | l | p | s |    (The letter **c** is introduced.)

Collect some pictures of animals that begin with **c** and **l** for the transfer activity.

**Make:**    as    pal    lap    sap    cap    clap    slap    caps    claps

**Sort:**

| as | cap | slap | pal | lap |
|----|-----|------|-----|-----|
|    | clap | sap |    |    |
|    | caps |    |    |    |
|    | claps |    |    |    |

**Transfer:**   (Show pictures or name animals that begin with today's letters.)

| cat | panda | lion | camel |
|-----|-------|------|-------|
| seal | alligator | ant | |
| cow | ladybug | pig | |

## Make Words

- Have children name and hold up letters.
- Tell children how many letters to use to make each word.
- Have children say each word and stretch out some words.
- Give sentences to clarify meaning.
- Give specific instructions on how to change words:
  — Add one letter.
  — Change the first letter.
  — Use the same letters.
- Have children clear their holders before making an unrelated word.
- Have children correct their word once it is made in the pocket chart.

## Sort Words

- Put words in pocket chart in the order made.
- Have children say and spell each word.
- Remind them of how each word was changed to spell the new word.
- Select one word beginning with each letter and line up in columns.
- Let children choose the other words that begin that way.
- Have children pronounce the words.

## Transfer Words

- Have children take their letters out of their holders.
- Point to some objects in the room that begin with these letters.
- Have children say the word and hold up the beginning letter.

# Lesson 9
## stamp

**Letters:** a m p s t (The letter **m** is introduced.)

Collect some pictures of foods that begin with **m**, **s**, and **t** for the transfer activity.

**Make:** as  am  at  sat  mat  map  tap  pat  past  stamp

**Sort:**

| | | | | |
|---|---|---|---|---|
| as | sat | mat | pat | tap |
| am | stamp | map | past | |
| at | | | | |

**Transfer:** (Show pictures or name foods that begin with today's letters.)

| | | | |
|---|---|---|---|
| soup | pizza | pie | peas |
| apples | tomatoes | muffins | |
| sandwich | tacos | macaroni | |

## Make Words

- Have children name and hold up letters.
- Tell children how many letters to use to make each word.
- Have children say each word and stretch out some words.
- Give sentences to clarify meaning.
- Give specific instructions on how to change words:
  — Add one letter.
  — Change the first letter.
  — Use the same letters.
- Have children clear their holders before making an unrelated word.
- Have children correct their word once it is made in the pocket chart.

## Sort Words

- Put words in pocket chart in the order made.
- Have children say and spell each word.
- Remind them of how each word was changed to spell the new word.
- Select one word beginning with each letter and line up in columns.
- Let children choose the other words that begin that way.
- Have children pronounce the words.

## Transfer Words

- Have children take their letters out of their holders.
- Point to some objects in the room that begin with these letters.
- Have children say the word and hold up the beginning letter.

# Lesson 10

## rafts

**Letters:** | a | | f | | r | | s | | t | (The letter **f** is introduced.)

Collect some pictures of animals that begin with **f** for the transfer activity.

**Make:**   as   at   rat   sat   fat   fast   rats   raft   rafts

**Sort:**

| | | | |
|---|---|---|---|
| as | rat | fat | sat |
| at | raft | fast | |
| | rafts | | |
| | rats | | |

**Transfer:** (Show pictures or name animals that begin with today's letters.)

| | | | |
|---|---|---|---|
| ant | tiger | rabbit | raccoon |
| seal | alligator | turtle | |
| fish | turtle | fox | |

## Make Words

- Have children name and hold up letters.
- Tell children how many letters to use to make each word.
- Have children say each word and stretch out some words.
- Give sentences to clarify meaning.
- Give specific instructions on how to change words:
  — Add one letter.
  — Change the first letter.
  — Use the same letters.
- Have children clear their holders before making an unrelated word.
- Have children correct their word once it is made in the pocket chart.

## Sort Words

- Put words in pocket chart in the order made.
- Have children say and spell each word.
- Remind them of how each word was changed to spell the new word.
- Select one word beginning with each letter and line up in columns.
- Let children choose the other words that begin that way.
- Have children pronounce the words.

## Transfer Words

- Have children take their letters out of their holders.
- Point to some objects in the room that begin with these letters.
- Have children say the word and hold up the beginning letter.

# Assessment Lessons 1-10

Assessment suggestions are given after every tenth lesson. All children may not be able to do everything on the assessment but they should all be showing growth in their blending, segmenting, and letter-sound knowledge. You may not need to do these assessments with every child. If you have children who you are *sure* can do these skills, there is no need to do the assessments.

The lessons so far have included the **vowel a and the consonants b, c, d, f, g, h, l, m, n, p, r, s, and t.** The letters **c**, **f**, **g**, **h**, and **m** were used in only one lesson and so it is too soon to assess children's knowledge of them. This assessment focuses on the names and common sounds for the letters **b, d, l, n, p, r, s,** and **t** and on the children's ability to segment words and blend sounds.

## Assess Letter Name and Sound Knowledge

Show each child a letter and ask that child to name that letter, tell you its common sound, and name a word that begins with that sound. Indicate the child's success by putting the date and a plus or minus in each box. Record in pencil so that you can change the plus to a minus and change the date when a child has demonstrated the three levels of knowledge with each letter. Check after lesson 10 for letters **a**, **b**, **d**, **l**, **n**, **p**, **r**, **s**, and **t**.

## Assess Blending and Segmenting

Determine if the child can segment by saying five of the words used in lessons 1–10 and asking the child to stretch these words for you. Model a few examples first to be sure each child understands the task. Words you might use are:

**sat   band   ant   at   past**

Determine if the child can blend by stretching out five of the words used in lessons 1–10 and asking the child to tell you the word. Model a few examples first to be sure each child understands the task. Words you might use are:

**ran   last   and   rag   trap**

Record each child's responses on a record sheet such as this.

Child's Name _____

| Letter | Name | Sound | Word | Segments | | Blends | | | |
|--------|------|-------|------|----------|---|--------|---|---|---|
| a | | | | sat | | ran | | | |
| d | | | | band | | last | | | |
| n | | | | ant | | and | | | |
| s | | | | rat | | rag | | | |
| b | | | | past | | trap | | | |
| t | | | | | | | | | |
| l | | | | | | | | | |
| r | | | | | | | | | |
| p | | | | | | | | | |

Here is one child's record sheet filled in after the assessment.

Child's Name ____Cooper_____

| Letter | Name | Sound | Word | Segments | | Blends | | | |
|--------|------|-------|------|----------|---|--------|---|---|---|
| a | 9/21 + | + | + | sat | 9/21 + | ran | 9/21 + | | |
| d | 9/21 + | + | + | band | 9/21 + | last | 9/21 - | | |
| n | 9/21 + | + | + | ant | 9/21 - | and | 9/21 + | | |
| s | 9/21 + | - | + | rat | 9/21 + | rag | 9/21 + | | |
| b | 9/21 + | + | + | past | 9/21 + | trap | 9/21 + | | |
| t | 9/21 + | + | + | | | | | | |
| l | 9/21 + | + | - | | | | | | |
| r | 9/21 + | + | + | | | | | | |
| p | 9/21 + | + | + | | | | | | |

# Lessons 11-20

These lessons provide more practice with segmenting and blending and with the most common consonants. They also teach the common sounds for the vowels **e**, **i**, **o**, and **u**.

# Lesson 11

## clamps

**Letters:** **a, c, l, m, p, s**   (The consonants **c, l, m, p, s** and the vowel **a** are reviewed.)

**Words to Make:** **am   Sam   Pam   map   cap   camp   lamp   lamps   clamps**

This is the first lesson that includes names. After children hold up and name their lower-case letters, have them show you the capital side they will use to spell a name.

## Part One ● Making Words

Have the children arrange their letters in front of their holders to match the pocket-chart letters, with the vowel first and the other letters in alphabetical order.

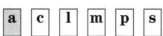

Begin the lesson by naming each pocket-chart letter. Ask the children to hold up their little letter cards as you hold up the large letter cards. Have them show both lowercase and capital letters. Tell students that they will be spelling two names in this lesson.

**am**  "The first word we are going to spell is **am**. I **am** your teacher. Everyone say **am**. Use 2 letters to spell **am**."

Look in the students' holders and choose a child who has **am** spelled correctly to spell **am** with the pocket-chart letters. Have the children chorally spell **am** after **am** is made with the pocket-chart letters and fix their word if it is not correct.

**Sam**  "The next word we are going to spell is **Sam**. I have a cousin named **Sam**. Everyone say **Sam**. Choose a letter and add it to **a-m** to spell the name **Sam**."

Look in the students' holders and choose a child who has **Sam** spelled with a capital **S** to spell **Sam** with the pocket-chart letters. Have the children chorally spell **Sam**.

**Pam**  "Take the **S** out of your holders and add a different letter to spell the name **Pam**. **Pam** is Sam's sister. Everyone say **Pam**.

Continue the lesson, giving children explicit instruction about which letters to remove and where to add letters. Put each word in a sentence and have children say each word before making it. Have them "stretch" words to provide practice for children who are still learning to segment words. Let a child who has spelled the word correctly come to the front of the room and make that word with the pocket-chart letters. Choose your struggling readers when the word is an easy word and choose your advanced readers for harder words. Have the children chorally spell each word after it is made in the pocket chart and fix their word to match.

| | |
|---|---|
| **map** | "Use the same letters in **Pam** to spell **map**. We like to find places on the **map**. Everyone say **map**." |
| **cap** | "Take the **m** out and use a different letter to spell **cap**. My son loves to wear his baseball **cap**. Everyone say **cap**." |
| **camp** | "Make space between the **a** and the **p** and add a letter to turn **cap** into **camp**. Many of you go to **camp** in the summer. Everyone say **camp**. Stretch the word **camp** and listen for which letter to add." |
| **lamp** | "Change the first letter in **camp** to spell **lamp**. Please turn on the **lamp**. Everyone say **lamp**." |
| **lamps** | "Add one letter to lamp to spell **lamps**. I have lots of **lamps** in my house. Everyone say **lamps**." |
| **clamps** | "We have one more word to spell. Add the **c** someplace in **lamps** to spell **clamps**. We use **clamps** to hold things together. Everyone say **clamps**." |

End the making words part of the lesson by having one child spell **clamps** with the pocket-chart letters and letting everyone hold up their holders to show you **clamps** made in their holders. Have them close the holders and turn their attention to the pocket chart.

# Part Two • Sorting Words (Sort for the letters **a**, **c**, **l**, **m**, **p**, and **s**.)

Tell your students that they are going to say all the words they spelled and then sort them according to the first letter. Using the index cards with the words, place them in the pocket chart and have the children pronounce them. Remind the children of what they changed to make each word as you put each word in the pocket chart.

"First we used 2 letters to spell **am**, **a-m**."

"We added the capital **S** to spell the name **Sam**, **S-a-m**."

"We changed the **S** to a **P** to spell another name **Pam**, **P-a-m**."

"We used the same letters in **Pam** spell **map**, **m-a-p**."

"We changed the first letter to spell **cap**, **c-a-p**."

"We added a letter to **cap** to spell **camp**, **c-a-m-p**."

"We changed the **c** to an **l** to spell **lamp**, **l-a-m-p**."

"We added an **s** to spell **lamps**, **l-a-m-p-s**."

"We added a **c** to change lamps into **clamps**, **c-l-a-m-p-s**."

Now choose six children—one for each letter—to come to the front of the room and sort the words according to the first letter.

| | | | | | |
|---|---|---|---|---|---|
| cap | am | lamp | map | Sam | Pam |
| camp | | lamps | | | |
| clamps | | | | | |

# Part Three • Transfer

The final step will take only a few minutes but is crucial if children are going to use the letter-sound relationships they are learning in the Making Words lessons.

Ask the children to open their letter holders and take out the letters and lay them down in front of their holder in the same order they had at the beginning of the lesson. Order the pocket-chart letters in the same way.

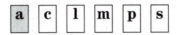

Use your food and animal pictures that begin with these letters. Be sure to have the children name the picture as they hold up the letter that word begins with.

# Lesson 12

## hunts

**Letters:** u  h  n  s  t   (The vowel **u** is introduced.)

Make sure you have an umbrella in the room for the transfer activity.

**Make:**  us  sun  nut  hut  huts  nuts  stun  hunt  hunts

**Sort:**

| us | hut | sun | nut |
|----|------|------|------|
|    | huts | stun | nuts |
|    | hunt |      |      |
|    | hunts |     |      |

**Transfer:** (Point to objects in the room that begin with today's letters.)

| umbrella | teeth | necks |
|----------|--------|---------|
| noses | teacher | scissors |
| hands | sink | notebooks |

# Make Words

- Have children name and hold up letters.
- Tell children how many letters to use to make each word.
- Have children say each word and stretch out some words.
- Give sentences to clarify meaning.
- Give specific instructions on how to change words:
  — Add one letter.
  — Change the first letter.
  — Use the same letters.
- Have children clear their holders before making an unrelated word.
- Have children correct their word once it is made in the pocket chart.

# Sort Words

- Put words in pocket chart in the order made.
- Have children say and spell each word.
- Remind them of how each word was changed to spell the new word.
- Select one word beginning with each letter and line up in columns.
- Let children choose the other words that begin that way.
- Have children pronounce the words.

# Transfer Words

- Have children take their letters out of their holders.
- Point to some objects in the room that begin with these letters.
- Have children say the word and hold up the beginning letter.

# Lesson 13

## stung

**Letters:**  u  g  n  s  t   (The vowel **u** is reviewed.)

Children have already made many of these words and should make them relatively quickly.

**Make:**   us   Gus   sun   gun   tug   nut   nuts   snug   sung   stung

**Sort:**

| us | sun | nut | Gus | tug |
|----|-----|-----|-----|-----|
|    | snug | nuts | gun |    |
|    | sung |     |     |    |
|    | stung |    |     |    |

**Transfer:**   (Point to objects in the room that begin with today's letters.)

| umbrella | noses | necks |
|----------|-------|-------|
| teeth | teacher | scissors |
| girls | sink | notebooks |

## Make Words

- Have children name and hold up letters.
- Tell children how many letters to use to make each word.
- Have children say each word and stretch out some words.
- Give sentences to clarify meaning.
- Give specific instructions on how to change words:
  — Add one letter.
  — Change the first letter.
  — Use the same letters.
- Have children clear their holders before making an unrelated word.
- Make sure children use their capital **G** when spelling the name **Gus**.
- Have children correct their word once it is made in the pocket chart.

## Sort Words

- Put words in pocket chart in the order made.
- Have children say and spell each word.
- Remind them of how each word was changed to spell the new word.
- Select one word beginning with each letter and line up in columns.
- Let children choose the other words that begin that way.
- Have children pronounce the words.

## Transfer Words

- Have children take their letters out of their holders.
- Point to some objects in the room that begin with these letters.
- Have children say the word and hold up the beginning letter.

## spend

**Letters:** e d n p s (The vowel **e** is introduced.)

**Make:** Ed Ned end den pen pens dens send spend

**Sort:**

| ed | pen | den | send | Ned |
|----|-----|-----|------|-----|
| end | pens | dens | spend | |

**Transfer:** (Point to objects that begin with today's letters.)

| envelope | desks | necks | elbows |
|----------|-------|-------|--------|
| noses | paper | scissors | door |
| pencils | sink | notebooks | |

## Make Words

- Have children name and hold up letters.
- Tell children how many letters to use to make each word.
- Have children say each word and stretch out some words.
- Give sentences to clarify meaning.
- Give specific instructions on how to change words:
  — Add one letter.
  — Change the first letter.
  — Use the same letters.
- Have children clear their holders before making an unrelated word.
- Make sure children use their capital letters when spelling the names **Ed** and **Ned**.
- Have children correct their word once it is made in the pocket chart.

## Sort Words

- Put words in pocket chart in the order made.
- Have children say and spell each word.
- Remind them of how each word was changed to spell the new word.
- Select one word beginning with each letter and line up in columns.
- Let children choose the other words that begin that way.
- Have children pronounce the words.

## Transfer Words

- Have children take their letters out of their holders.
- Point to objects in the room that begin with these letters.
- Have children say the word and hold up the beginning letter.

# Lesson 15

## spent

**Letters:** e n p s t (The vowel **e** is reviewed.)

Children have already made many of these words and should make them relatively quickly.

**Make:** pen ten net pet pets step pest nest sent spent

**Sort:**

| pen | sent | net | ten |
|-----|------|------|-----|
| pet | spent | nest | |
| pets | step | | |
| pest | | | |

**Transfer:** (Point to objects that begin with today's letters.)

| envelope | socks | necks | elbows |
|----------|-------|-------|--------|
| noses | paper | teeth | teacher |
| pencils | sink | notebooks | |

## Make Words

- Have children name and hold up letters.
- Tell children how many letters to use to make each word.
- Have children say each word and stretch out some words.
- Give sentences to clarify meaning.
- Give specific instructions on how to change words:
  — Add one letter.
  — Change the first letter.
  — Use the same letters.
- Have children clear their holders before making an unrelated word.
- Have children correct their word once it is made in the pocket chart.

## Sort Words

- Put words in pocket chart in the order made.
- Have children say and spell each word.
- Remind them of how each word was changed to spell the new word.
- Select one word beginning with each letter and line up in columns.
- Let children choose the other words that begin that way.
- Have children pronounce the words.

## Transfer Words

- Have children take their letters out of their holders.
- Point to objects in the room that begin with these letters.
- Have children say the word and hold up the beginning letter.

# Lesson 16

## print

**Letters:** i n p r t (The vowel **i** is introduced.)

For the transfer, you will need a picture of insects—several different kinds in one picture.

**Make:** it   in   tin   pin   pit   tip   nip   rip   trip   print

**Sort:**

| it | tin | pin | nip | rip |
|----|-----|-----|-----|-----|
| in | tip | pit | | |
| | trip | print | | |

**Transfer:** Food and animal pictures, including insects, beginning with **i**, **t**, **n**, **p**, and **r**

## Make Words

- Have children name and hold up letters.
- Tell children how many letters to use to make each word.
- Have children say each word and stretch out some words.
- Give sentences to clarify meaning.
- Give specific instructions on how to change words:
  — Add one letter.
  — Change the first letter.
  — Use the same letters.
- Have children clear their holders before making an unrelated word.
- Have children correct their word once it is made in the pocket chart.

## Sort Words

- Put words in pocket chart in the order made.
- Have children say and spell each word.
- Remind them of how each word was changed to spell the new word.
- Select one word beginning with each letter and line up in columns.
- Let children choose the other words that begin that way.
- Have children pronounce the words.

## Transfer Words

- Have childres take their letters out of their holders.
- Add a picture of insects and use your pictures of food and animals that begin with these letters.
- Have children say the word and hold up the beginning letter.

# Lesson 17

## trips

**Letters:** | i | | p | | r | | s | | t |   (The vowel **i** is reviewed.)

Children have already made many of these words and should make them relatively quickly.

**Make:**   is   it   sit   pit   tip   sip   rip   trip   strip   trips

**Sort:**

| is | sit | tip | pit | rip |
|---|---|---|---|---|
| it | sit | trip | | |
| | strip | trips | | |

**Transfer:** Food and animal pictures, including insects, beginning with **i**, **t**, **s**, **p**, and **r**

## Make Words

- Have children name and hold up letters.
- Tell children how many letters to use to make each word.
- Have children say each word and stretch out some words.
- Give sentences to clarify meaning.
- Give specific instructions on how to change words:
  — Add one letter.
  — Change the first letter.
  — Use the same letters.
- Have children clear their holders before making an unrelated word.
- Have children correct their word once it is made in the pocket chart.

## Sort Words

- Put words in pocket chart in the order made.
- Have children say and spell each word.
- Remind them of how each word was changed to spell the new word.
- Select one word beginning with each letter and line up in columns.
- Let children choose the other words that begin that way.
- Have children pronounce the words.

## Transfer Words

- Have children take their letters out of their holders.
- Show children some pictures of food and animals that begin with these letters.
- Have children say the word and hold up the beginning letter.

# Lesson 18

## gifts

**Letters:** | i | f | g | s | t |  (The vowel **i** is reviewed.)

**Make:**   is   if   it   sit   fit   fist   sift   gift   gifts

**Sort:**

| is | sit | fit | gift |
|----|-----|------|-------|
| it | sift | fist | gifts |
| if | | | |

**Transfer:** Food and animal pictures, including insects, beginning with **i**, **t**, **s**, **p**, and **r**

## Make Words

- Have children name and hold up letters.
- Tell children how many letters to use to make each word.
- Have children say each word and stretch out some words.
- Give sentences to clarify meaning.
- Give specific instructions on how to change words:
    — Add one letter.
    — Change the first letter.
    — Use the same letters.
- Have children clear their holders before making an unrelated word.
- Have children correct their word once it is made in the pocket chart.

## Sort Words

- Put words in pocket chart in the order made.
- Have children say and spell each word.
- Remind them of how each word was changed to spell the new word.
- Select one word beginning with each letter and line up in columns.
- Let children choose the other words that begin that way.
- Have children pronounce the words.

## Transfer Words

- Have children take their letters out of their holders.
- Show children some pictures of food and animals that begin with these letters.
- Have children say the word and hold up the beginning letter.

# Lesson 19

## plots

**Letters:** | o | l | p | s | t | (The vowel **o** is introduced.)

You will need pictures of olives and oranges for the transfer.

**Make:** top  pot  lot  slot  spot  stop  tops  tap  pots  lots  plot  plots

**Sort:**

| top | pot | lot | slot |
|-----|-----|-----|------|
| tops | pots | lots | spot |
| tap | plot | | stop |
| | plots | | |

**Transfer:** Food and animal pictures, including olives and oranges, beginning with **o**, **t**, **p**, **s**, and **l**

## Make Words

- Have children name and hold up letters.
- Tell children how many letters to use to make each word.
- Have children say each word and stretch out some words.
- Give sentences to clarify meaning.
- Give specific instructions on how to change words:
  — Add one letter.
  — Change the first letter.
  — Use the same letters.
- Have children clear their holders before making an unrelated word.
- Have children correct their word once it is made in the pocket chart.

## Sort Words

- Put words in pocket chart in the order made.
- Have children say and spell each word.
- Remind them of how each word was changed to spell the new word.
- Select one word beginning with each letter and line up in columns.
- Let children choose the other words that begin that way.
- Have children pronounce the words.

## Transfer Words

- Have children take their letters out of their holders.
- Show children some pictures of food and animals that begin with these letters.
- Have children say the word and hold up the beginning letter.

# Lesson 20
## stomp

**Letters:** `o` `m` `p` `s` `t`  (The vowel **o** is reviewed.)

Children have already made many of these words and should make them relatively quickly.

**Make:**  Tom  pot  top  mop  mops  tops  pots  spot  stop  stomp

**Sort:**

| Tom | pot | spot | mop |
|-----|-----|------|-----|
| top | pots | stop | mops |
| tops | | stomp | |

**Transfer:**  Food and animal pictures, including olives and oranges, beginning with **o**, **t**, **p**, **s**, and **l**

## Make Words

- Have children name and hold up letters.
- Tell children how many letters to use to make each word.
- Have children say each word and stretch out some words.
- Give sentences to clarify meaning.
- Give specific instructions on how to change words:
  — Add one letter.
  — Change the first letter.
  — Use the same letters.
- Have children clear their holders before making an unrelated word.
- Make sure children use their capital **T** when spelling the name **Tom**.
- Have children correct their word once it is made in the pocket chart.

## Sort Words

- Put words in pocket chart in the order made.
- Have children say and spell each word.
- Remind them of how each word was changed to spell the new word.
- Select one word beginning with each letter and line up in columns.
- Let children choose the other words that begin that way.
- Have children pronounce the words.

## Transfer Words

- Have children take their letters out of their holders.
- Show children some pictures of food and animals that begin with these letters.
- Have children say the word and hold up the beginning letter.

# Assessment Lessons 11-20

The lessons so far have included the **common sounds for the vowels a, e, i, o, and u and the consonants b, c, d, f, g, h, l, m, n, p, r, s, and t.** All consonants have been used in at least two lessons. This assessment focuses on the names and common sounds for these letters and on the children's ability to segment words and blend sound. As with all assessments, there is no need to do them with children you are *sure* can do the skill. All the short vowels are being introduced, but it is too soon to expect all the children to know them. They will be assessed after the children have had a chance to contrast these vowels in later lessons.

| Letter | Name | Sound | Word | Segments | | Blends | |
|--------|------|-------|------|----------|---|--------|---|
| **After Lesson 10** | | | | | | | |
| a | | | | sat | | ran | |
| d | | | | band | | last | |
| n | | | | ant | | and | |
| s | | | | rat | | rag | |
| b | | | | past | | trap | |
| t | | | | | | | |
| l | | | | | | | |
| r | | | | | | | |
| p | | | | | | | |
| **After Lesson 20** | | | | | | | |
| c | | | | nut | | tug | |
| f | | | | hunt | | send | |
| g | | | | pet | | pest | |
| h | | | | pin | | trip | |
| m | | | | spot | | mop | |
| | | | | | | | |
| | | | | | | | |

## Assess Letter Name and Sound Knowledge

Use the procedure described after lesson 5 to determine children's knowledge of letter names, sounds, and words for the letters **c**, **f**, **g**, **h**, and **m**. Recheck any children on letters they had not learned after lesson 10.

## Assess Blending and Segmenting

Determine if the child can segment by saying words used in these lessons and asking the child to stretch these words for you. Model a few examples first to be sure each child understands the task. Words you might use are:

**nut   hunt   pet   pin   spot**

Determine if the child can blend by stretching out words used in these first lessons and asking the child to tell you the word. Model a few examples first to be sure each child understands the task. Words you might use are:

**tug   send   pest   trip   mop**

# Lessons 21-30

These lessons provide more practice with segmenting and blending as well as reviews of vowel and consonant sounds. The consonant **k** and the letter combinations **ch**, **sh**, **th**, and **ck** are introduced.

---

## Lesson 21
## think

**Letters:**   **i, h, k, n, t**   (The consonant combination **th** is introduced.)

**Words to Make:**   **it   in   ink   tin   kit   hit   hint   thin   think**

## Part One • Making Words

 Have the children arrange their letters in front of their holders to match the pocket-chart letters, with the vowel first and the other letters in alphabetical order.

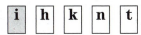

Begin the lesson by naming each pocket-chart letter. Ask the children to hold up their little letter cards as you hold up the large letter cards. After naming the letters, have them hold up their **t** and **h** and tell them that these two letters together make the sound you hear at the beginning of **thumbs**. Have them wiggle their thumbs and make the **th** sound.

**it**      "The first word we are going to spell is **it**. Take a letter and put **it** in the holder. Everyone say **it**. Use 2 letters to spell **it**."

Look in the students' holders and choose a child who has **it** spelled correctly to spell **it** with the pocket-chart letters. Have the children chorally spell **it** after **it** is made with the pocket-chart letters and fix their word if it is not correct.

**in**      "The next word we are going to spell is **in**. We are **in** our classroom. Everyone say **in**. Change the last letter in **it** to spell **in**."

Look in the students' holders and choose a child who has **in** spelled correctly to spell **in** with the pocket-chart letters. Have the children chorally spell **in** after **in** is made.

**ink**      "Add a letter to **i-n** to spell **ink**. My red pen has red **ink** in it. Everyone say **ink**."

Continue the lesson, giving children explicit instruction about which letters to re-move and where to add letters. Put each word in a sentence and have children say each word before making it. Have them "stretch" words to provide practice for children who are still learning to segment words. Let a child who has spelled the word correctly come to the front of the room and make that word with the pocket-chart letters. Choose your struggling readers when the word is an easy word and choose your advanced readers for harder words. Have the children chorally spell each word after it is made in the pocket chart and fix their word to match.

**tin**      "Clear your holders and spell another 3 letter word, **tin**. The cups we drink from when we are camping are made of **tin**. Everyone say **tin**."

**kit**      "Clear your holders again and spell another 3 letter word, **kit**. My son built a model airplane from a **kit**. Everyone say **kit**."

**hit**      "Change just the first letter to spell **hit**. The batter **hit** the ball and ran to first base. Everyone say **hit**."

**hint**      "Add 1 letter to **hit** to spell **hint**. I can't tell you what you are getting for your birthday but I can give you a **hint**. Everyone say **hint**. Stretch the word **hint** and listen for which letter to add and where to add it."

**thin**      "Use the same 4 letters in **hint** but move them around to spell **thin**. I like pizza with **thin** crust. Everyone say **thin**. Wiggle your thumbs and think about how to spell **thin**."

**think**      "We have one more word to spell. Add the **k** to **thin** to spell **think**. I **think** you are all very good at making words. Everyone say **think**."

End the making words part of the lesson by having one child spell **think** with the pocket-chart letters and letting everyone hold up their holders to show you **think** made in their holders. Have them close the holders and turn their attention to the pocket chart.

## Part Two • Sorting Words (Sort for the letters sounds **i**, **h**, **k**, **t**, and **th**.)

Tell your students that they are going to say all the words they spelled and then sort them according to the first letter. Using the index cards with the words, place them in the pocket chart and have the children pronounce them. Remind the children of what they changed to make each word as you put each word in the pocket chart.

"First we used 2 letters to spell **it**, **i-t**."

"We changed the **t** to an **n** to spell **in**, **i-n**."

"We added the **k** to **in** to spell **ink**, **i-n-k**."

"We started over and spelled **tin**, **t-i-n**."

"We started over again and spelled **kit**, **k-i-t**."

"We changed the **k** to an **h** to spell **hit**, **h-i-t**."

"We added an **n** before the **t** to spell **hint**, **h-i-n-t**."

"We used the same letters to spell **thin**, **t-h-i-n**."

"We added a **k** to change **thin** into **think**, **t-h-i-n-k**."

Now choose five children to sort the word according to the first letter. Help them put **thin** and **think** in a separate column and remind them that **th** together makes the sound they hear when they say thumbs.

| | | | | |
|---|---|---|---|---|
| **in** | **hit** | **kit** | **tin** | **thin** |
| **it** | **hint** | | | **think** |
| **ink** | | | | |

# Part Three • Transfer

Ask the children to open their letter holders and take out the letters and lay them down in front of their holders in the same order they had at the beginning of the lesson. Order the pocket-chart letters in the same way.

Name things in the room that begin with these letters and have students point to them and name them. Tell them that some of the words begin like the word **thumbs** and they will need to hold up their **t** and their **h** when they hear the **th** sound. Here are some things you are likely to have in your classroom. Include other things you notice that aren't listed here.

| | | | |
|---|---|---|---|
| **thumbs** | **noses** | **hands** | **kids** |
| **teacher** | **hair** | **teeth** | **necks** |
| **three** | **thirteen** | **keys** | |

# Lesson 22
## thanks

**Letters:** a  h  k  n  s  t  (The consonant combination **th** is reviewed.)

**Make:**  at  sat  hat  Nat  tan  than  sank  Hank  tank  thank  thanks

**Sort:**

| at | hat | Nat | sat | tan | than |
|---|---|---|---|---|---|
|  | Hank |  | sank | tank | thank |
|  |  |  |  |  | thanks |

**Transfer:** (Point to objects that begin with today's letters.)

| thumbs | noses | hands | kids |
|---|---|---|---|
| teacher | hair | sink | thermostat |
| three | thirteen | keys | alphabet |

## Make Words

- Have children name and hold up letters. Have them hold up the **t** and the **h** and wiggle their **thumbs**.
- Tell children how many letters to use to make each word.
- Have children say each word and stretch out some words.
- Give sentences to clarify meaning.
- Give specific instructions on how to change words:
  — Add one letter.
  — Change the first letter.
  — Use the same letters.
- Have children clear their holders before making an unrelated word.
- Make sure children use a capital letter when spelling the names **Nat** and **Hank**.
- Have children correct their word once it is made in the pocket chart.

## Sort Words

- Put words in pocket chart in the order made.
- Have children say and spell each word.
- Remind them of how each word was changed to spell the new word.
- Select one word beginning with each letter and line up in columns.
- Let children choose the other words that begin that way.
- Have children pronounce the words.

## Transfer Words

- Have children take their letters out of their holders.
- Point to objects in the room that begin with these letters.
- Have children say the word and hold up the beginning letter.

# Lesson 23

## shrimp

**Letters:**  | i | h | m | p | r | s |   (The consonant combination **sh** is introduced.)

Have children hold up their **s** and **h** and shake their shoulders.

**Make:**   is   his   him   rim   rip   hip   sip   ship   shrimp

**Sort:**

| is | his | rim | sip | ship |
|----|-----|-----|-----|------|
|    | him | rip |     | shrimp |
|    | hip |     |     |       |

**Transfer:**   (Point to objects that begin with today's letters.)

| shoulders | sink | shelf | paper |
|-----------|------|-------|-------|
| pencil | hands | scissors | hair |
| shirt | sink | ruler | |

## Make Words

- Have children name and hold up letters. Have them hold up the **s** and the **h** and shrug their shoulders.
- Tell children how many letters to use to make each word.
- Have children say each word and stretch out some words.
- Give sentences to clarify meaning.
- Give specific instructions on how to change words:
  — Add one letter.
  — Change the first letter.
  — Use the same letters.
- Have children clear their holders before making an unrelated word.
- Make sure children use their capital **G** when spelling the name **Gus**.
- Have children correct their word once it is made in the pocket chart.

## Sort Words

- Put words in pocket chart in the order made.
- Have children say and spell each word.
- Remind them of how each word was changed to spell the new word.
- Select one word beginning with each letter and line up in columns.
- Let children choose the other words that begin that way.
- Have children pronounce the words.

## Transfer Words

- Have children take their letters out of their holders.
- Point to objects in the room that begin with these letters.
- Have children say the word and hold up the beginning letter.

## shrink

**Letters:**  i h k n r s (The consonant combination **sh** is reviewed.)

 **Make:**  in  is  his  ink  sink  skin  rink  risk  shrink

 **Sort:**

| in | sink | rink | his | shrink |
|----|------|------|-----|--------|
| is | skin | risk | | |
| ink | | | | |

**Transfer:** (Point to objects that begin with today's letters.)

| shoulders | sink | shelf | keys |
|-----------|------|-------|------|
| kids | hands | scissors | hair |
| shirt | sink | ruler | noses |

## Make Words

- Have children name and hold up letters. Have them hold up the **s** and the **h** and shrug their shoulders.
- Tell children how many letters to use to make each word.
- Have children say each word and stretch out some words.
- Give sentences to clarify meaning.
- Give specific instructions on how to change words:
  — Add one letter.
  — Change the first letter.
  — Use the same letters.
- Have children clear their holders before making an unrelated word.
- Make sure children use their capital letters when spelling the names **Ed** and **Ned**.
- Have children correct their word once it is made in the pocket chart.

## Sort Words

- Put words in pocket chart in the order made.
- Have children say and spell each word.
- Remind them of how each word was changed to spell the new word.
- Select one word beginning with each letter and line up in columns.
- Let children choose the other words that begin that way.
- Have children pronounce the words.

## Transfer Words

- Have children take their letters out of their holders.
- Point to objects in the room that begin with these letters.
- Have children say the word and hold up the beginning letter.

# Lesson 25

## champs

**Letters:** | a | c | h | m | p | s |  (The consonant combination **ch** is introduced.)

Have children hold up their **c** and **h** and point to their chin and cheeks.

**Make:**  as  has  ash  cap  map  mash  cash  camp  camps  champ  champs

**Sort:**

| as | has | map | cash | champ |
|----|-----|-----|------|-------|
| ash | | mash | camp | champs |
| | | | camps | |
| | | | cap | |

**Transfer:** (Point to objects that begin with today's letters.)

| alphabet | socks | cheeks | chair |
|----------|-------|--------|-------|
| chins | paper | hands | computer |
| pencils | sink | notebooks | carpet |

## Make Words

- Have children name and hold up letters. Have them hold up the **c** and the **h** and point to their chin and cheeks.
- Tell children how many letters to use to make each word.
- Have children say each word and stretch out some words.
- Give sentences to clarify meaning.
- Give specific instructions on how to change words:
  — Add one letter.
  — Change the first letter.
  — Use the same letters.
- Have children clear their holders before making an unrelated word.
- Have children correct their word once it is made in the pocket chart.

## Sort Words

- Put words in pocket chart in the order made.
- Have children say and spell each word.
- Remind them of how each word was changed to spell the new word.
- Select one word beginning with each letter and line up in columns.
- Let children choose the other words that begin that way.
- Have children pronounce the words.

## Transfer Words

- Have children take their letters out of their holders.
- Point to objects in the room that begin with these letters.
- Have children say the word and hold up the beginning letter.

## chimps

**Letters:** | i | | c | | h | | m | | p | | s |   (The consonant combinations **sh** and **ch** are reviewed.)

**Make:**   is   his   him   hip   sip   ship   chip   chimp   chimps

**Sort:**

| is | his | sip | ship | chip |
|----|-----|-----|------|------|
|    | hip |     |      | chimp |
|    | him |     |      | chimps |

**Transfer:**   (Point to objects that begin with today's letters.)

| hands | socks | cheeks | chair |
|-------|-------|--------|-------|
| chins | paper | cupboard | computer |
| pencils | sink | notebooks | carpet |

## Make Words

- Have children name and hold up letters. Have them hold up the **c** and the **h** and point to their chin and cheeks.
- Tell children how many letters to use to make each word.
- Have children say each word and stretch out some words.
- Give sentences to clarify meaning.
- Give specific instructions on how to change words:
  — Add one letter.
  — Change the first letter.
  — Use the same letters.
- Have children clear their holders before making an unrelated word.
- Have children correct their word once it is made in the pocket chart.

## Sort Words

- Put words in pocket chart in the order made.
- Have children say and spell each word.
- Remind them of how each word was changed to spell the new word.
- Select one word beginning with each letter and line up in columns.
- Let children choose the other words that begin that way.
- Have children pronounce the words.

## Transfer Words

- Have children take their letters out of their holders.
- Point to objects in the room that begin with these letters.
- Have children say the word and hold up the beginning letter.

# Lesson 27
## stack

**Letters:** | a | c | k | s | t |  (The consonant combination **ck** is introduced.)

Have children hold up their **c** and **k** and tell them that they will make some words that end with these two letters.

**Make:**  at  sat  cat  act  acts  cats  scat  sack  tack  tacks  stack

**Sort:**

| at | cat | sat | tack |
| act | cats | scat | tacks |
| acts | | sack | |
| | | stack | |

**Transfer:**  Food and animal pictures beginning with **a**, **c**, **s**, and **t**

# Make Words

- Have children name and hold up letters.
- Tell children how many letters to use to make each word.
- Have children say each word and stretch out some words.
- Give sentences to clarify meaning.
- Give specific instructions on how to change words:
  — Add one letter.
  — Change the first letter.
  — Use the same letters.
- Have children clear their holders before making an unrelated word.
- Have children correct their word once it is made in the pocket chart.

# Sort Words

- Put words in pocket chart in the order made.
- Have children say and spell each word.
- Remind them of how each word was changed to spell the new word.
- Select one word beginning with each letter and line up in columns.
- Let children choose the other words that begin that way.
- Have children pronounce the words.

# Transfer Words

- Have children take their letters out of their holders.
- Show children some pictures of food and animals that begin with these letters.
- Have children say the word and hold up the beginning letter.

# Lesson 28
## tracks

**Letters:** | a | c | k | r | s | t |   (The letters **a**, **c**, **k**, **r**, **s**, and **t** are reviewed.)

**Make:**  at  sat  rat  cat  scat  sack  rack  tack  stack  track  tracks

**Sort:**

| at | sat | rat | tack | cat |
|----|------|------|-------|-----|
|    | scat | rack | track |     |
|    | sack |      | tracks |    |
|    | stack |     |        |    |

**Transfer:** Food and animal pictures beginning with **a**, **c**, **r**, **s**, and **t**

## Make Words

- Have children name and hold up letters.
- Tell children how many letters to use to make each word.
- Have children say each word and stretch out some words.
- Give sentences to clarify meaning.
- Give specific instructions on how to change words:
  — Add one letter.
  — Change the first letter.
  — Use the same letters.
- Have children clear their holders before making an unrelated word.
- Have children correct their word once it is made in the pocket chart.

## Sort Words

- Put words in pocket chart in the order made.
- Have children say and spell each word.
- Remind them of how each word was changed to spell the new word.
- Select one word beginning with each letter and line up in columns.
- Let children choose the other words that begin that way.
- Have children pronounce the words.

## Transfer Words

- Have children take their letters out of their holders.
- Show children some pictures of food and animals that begin with these letters.
- Have children say the word and hold up the beginning letter.

## tricks

**Letters:** i  c  k  r  s  t  (The letters **i**, **c**, **k**, **r**, **s**, and **t** are reviewed. )

**Make:**  is  it  kit  sit  sick  Rick  tick  ticks  stick  trick  tricks

**Sort:**

| is | sit | kit | tick | Rick |
|----|------|-----|-------|------|
| it | sick | | ticks | |
| | stick | | trick | |
| | | | tricks | |

**Transfer:**  Food and animal pictures beginning with **i**, **c**, **r**, **s** and **t**

## Make Words

- Have children name and hold up letters.
- Tell children how many letters to use to make each word.
- Have children say each word and stretch out some words.
- Give sentences to clarify meaning.
- Give specific instructions on how to change words:
  — Add one letter.
  — Change the first letter.
  — Use the same letters.
- Have children clear their holders before making an unrelated word.
- Make sure children use their capital **R** when spelling the name **Rick**.
- Have children correct their word once it is made in the pocket chart.

## Sort Words

- Put words in pocket chart in the order made.
- Have children say and spell each word.
- Remind them of how each word was changed to spell the new word.
- Select one word beginning with each letter and line up in columns.
- Let children choose the other words that begin that way.
- Have children pronounce the words.

## Transfer Words

- Have children take their letters out of their holders.
- Show children some pictures of food and animals that begin with these letters.
- Have children say the word and hold up the beginning letter.

# Lesson 30
## trucks

**Letters:** | u | c | k | r | s | t |   (The letters **u**, **c**, **k**, **r**, **s**, and **t** are reviewed.)

Children have already made many of these words and should make them relatively quickly.

**Make:**   us   cut   rut   ruts   cuts   tuck   stuck   truck   trucks   struck

**Sort:**

| us | cut | stuck | rut | tuck |
|----|-----|-------|-----|------|
|    | cuts | struck | ruts | truck |
|    |     |       |     | trucks |

**Transfer:**   (Point to objects that begin with today's letters.)

| umbrella | scissors | kids | teeth |
|----------|----------|------|-------|
| noses | teacher | carpet | computer |
| socks | sink | keys | ruler |

## Make Words

- Have children name and hold up letters.
- Tell children how many letters to use to make each word.
- Have children say each word and stretch out some words.
- Give sentences to clarify meaning.
- Give specific instructions on how to change words:
  — Add one letter.
  — Change the first letter.
  — Use the same letters.
- Have children clear their holders before making an unrelated word.
- Make sure children use their capital **T** when spelling the name **Tom**.
- Have children correct their word once it is made in the pocket chart.

## Sort Words

- Put words in pocket chart in the order made.
- Have children say and spell each word.
- Remind them of how each word was changed to spell the new word.
- Select one word beginning with each letter and line up in columns.
- Let children choose the other words that begin that way.
- Have children pronounce the words.

## Transfer Words

- Have children take their letters out of their holders.
- Point to objects in the room that begin with these letters.
- Have children say the word and hold up the beginning letter.

# Assessment Lessons 21-30

The lessons so far have included the **common sounds for the vowels a, e, i, o, and u and the consonants b, c, d, f, g, h, k, l, m, n, p, r, s, and t and the digraphs sh, ch, and th.** *This assessment will focus on the names and common sounds for **sh**, **ch**, and **th** and on the children's ability to segment words and blend sounds.* This will be the final planned assessment for blending and segmenting. But you may want to continue to assess this for children who have not yet demonstrated they can blend and segment.

| Letter | Name | Sound | Word | Segments | | Blends | |
|--------|------|-------|------|----------|---|--------|---|
| **After Lesson 10** | | | | | | | |
| a | | | | sat | | ran | |
| d | | | | band | | last | |
| n | | | | ant | | and | |
| s | | | | rat | | rag | |
| b | | | | past | | trap | |
| t | | | | | | | |
| l | | | | | | | |
| r | | | | | | | |
| p | | | | | | | |
| **After Lesson 20** | | | | | | | |
| c | | | | nut | | tug | |
| f | | | | hunt | | send | |
| g | | | | pet | | pest | |
| h | | | | pin | | trip | |
| m | | | | spot | | mop | |
| **After Lesson 30** | | | | | | | |
| sh | | | | ship | | chip | |
| ch | | | | mash | | cash | |
| th | | | | than | | thin | |

## Assess Letter Name and Sound Knowledge:

Show the children cards on which you have written **sh**, **ch**, and **th**. Then ask them to name the two letters and tell you what sound these letters make. Ask them to tell you any words they know that begin with **sh**, **ch**, and **th**. Recheck any children on letters they had not learned after lesson 20.

## Assess Blending and Segmenting

Determine if the child can segment by saying words used in these lessons and asking the child to stretch these words for you. Model a few examples first to be sure each child understands the task. Words you might use are:

**ship    mash    than**

Determine if the child can blend by stretching out three of the words used in these first lessons and asking the child to tell you the word. Model a few examples first to be sure each child understands the task. Words you might use are:

**chip    cash    thin**

# Lessons 31-40

These lessons, which include two vowels, teach students how similar words are made by changing the vowel. They also teach the children the sounds for **w** and **j**. Beginning with lesson 31, students sort the words according to rhymes. In the transfer step, they use the rhyming words to spell three new rhyming words. This lesson introduces the concept of the "secret word." Remind your children that the last word in every lesson uses all the letters. Explain that today you will not tell them the last word; rather, they should try to figure it out on their own.

## Lesson 31

### wishing

**Letters:**   **i**, **i**, **g**, **h**, **n**, **s**, and **w**   (The vowel sound for **i** is reviewed.)

**Words to Make:**   in   is   his   wig   win   wins   wish   wing   sing   swing   wings   wishing

## Part One • Making Words

Have the children arrange their letters in front of their holders to match the pocket-chart letters, with the vowels first and the other letters in alphabetical order.

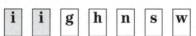

Begin the lesson by having children hold up and name each letter.

**in**      "The first word we are going to spell is **in**. You are **in** first grade. Everyone say **in**. Use 2 letters to spell **in**."

Choose a child who has **in** spelled correctly to spell **in** with the pocket-chart letters. Have the class chorally spell **in** and fix their word if **in** is not correct.

**is**      "The next word we are going to spell is **is**. This **is** our classroom. Everyone say **is**. Change the last letter to spell **is**."

Let a child who has **is** spelled correctly spell **is** with the pocket-chart letters.

**his**      "Add a letter to **is** to spell **his**. Carl has **his** red shirt on today. Everyone say **his**."

Continue the lesson, giving children explicit instruction about which letters to remove and where to add letters. Put each word in a sentence and have children say each word before making it. Have them "stretch" some words to provide practice for children who are still learning to segment words. Let a child who has spelled the word correctly come to the front of the room and make that word with the pocket-chart letters. Choose your struggling readers when the word is an easy word and choose your advanced readers for harder words. Have the children chorally spell each word after it is made in the pocket chart and fix their word to match.

| | |
|---|---|
| **wig** | "Clear your holders and spell another 3 letter word, **wig**. Do you know anyone who wears a **wig**? Everyone say **wig**." |
| **win** | "Change just the last letter to spell **win**. I hope our team will **win** the game. Everyone say **win**." |
| **wins** | "Add a letter to spell **wins**. When our team **wins**, we are happy. Everyone say **wins**." |
| **wish** | "Change the last 2 letters to spell **wish**. I make a **wish** on my birthday and then I blow out the candles. Everyone say **wish**." |
| **wing** | "Change the last 2 letters again to spell **wing**. The bird could not fly because her **wing** was broken. Everyone say **wing**." |
| **sing** | "Change the first letter to spell **sing**. We can all **sing**. Everyone say **sing**." |
| **swing** | "Add a letter to **sing** to spell **swing**. I will push you on the **swing**. Everyone say **swing**. Stretch out the sounds to figure out what to add to change **sing** to **swing**." |
| **wishing** | **(the secret word)** "We have one more word to spell. It is the word that uses all the letters—the secret word. Move your letters in your holder and see if you can figure out the secret word. Signal me if you think you have it." |

If no one makes the secret word in one minute, give them a clue.

"You can spell our secret word if you spell **wish** and then add the other letters at the end."

End the making words part of the lesson by having one child spell **wishing** in the pocket chart and letting everyone hold up their holders to show you **wishing** made in their holders. Have them close the holders and turn their attention to the pocket chart.

# Part Two • Sorting Words (Sort for the rhymes is, ing, and in.)

Tell your students that they are going to say all the words they spelled and then sort the rhyming words. Using the index cards with the words, place them in the pocket chart and have the children pronounce them. Remind the children of what they changed to make each word.

"First we used 2 letters to spell in, **i-n**."

"We changed the **n** to an **s** to spell is, **i-s**."

"We added the **h** to **is** to spell **his**, **h-i-s**."

"We started over and spelled **wig**, **w-i-g**."

"We changed the last letter and spelled **win**, **w-i-n**."

"We added the **s** to spell **wins**, **w-i-n-s**."

"We changed the last 2 letters to spell **wish**, **w-i-s-h**."

"We changed the last 2 letters again to spell **wing**, **w-i-n-g**."

"We changed the first letter to spell **sing**, **s-i-n-g**."

"We added the **w** to change sing into **swing**, **s-w-i-n-g**."

"Our secret word today was **wishing**, **w-i-s-h-i-n-g**."

"Today, we are going to sort out the rhymes. I will take one of each set and you can come and help me find the others."

Arrange one of each set of rhyming words to begin three columns.

**is**        **sing**        **win**

Choose three children and help them choose the rhyming words and line them up in columns. Have the rhyming words pronounced and have children notice that they all rhyme and they all have the same letters from the vowel to the end of the word.

**is**        **sing**        **win**

**his**      **wing**      **in**

**swing**

# Part Three • Transfer    spin   sting   chin

Have the children take out paper. Tell them that you are going to say a word that someone might be writing. By figuring out the rhyming pattern, they will be able to spell the word.

"The first word we will spell is **spin**. Tracy might be writing that she likes to **spin** around and get dizzy. Let's all say **spin** and listen for the two beginning letters."

Write **s-p** on an index card. Take the index card to the pocket chart and have the children pronounce **spin** with each set of rhyming words. When they decide that **spin** rhymes with **win** and **in**, write **i-n** next to **s-p**. Have the children write **spin** on their papers.

Repeat this procedure for **sting** and **chin**.

# Lesson 32
## jumping

**Letters:** | i | u | g | j | m | n | p |  (The letter **j** is introduced.)

**Make:**   in   pin   pig   pug   jug   mug   gum   ump   jump   jumping

**Sort:**
| in | pug | ump |
|----|-----|-----|
| pin | jug | jump |

**Transfer:**   chin   stump   bug

## Make Words

- Have children name and hold up letters.
- Tell children how many letters to use to make each word.
- Have children say each word and stretch out some words.
- Give sentences to clarify meaning.
- Give specific instructions on how to change words:
  — Add one letter.
  — Change the first letter.
  — Use the same letters.
- Have children clear their holders before making an unrelated word.
- Have children correct their word once it is made in the pocket chart.
- Give children one minute to figure out the secret word and then give them clues.

## Sort Words

- Put words in pocket chart in the order made.
- Have children say and spell each word.
- Remind them of how each word was changed to spell the new word.
- Select one word from each rhyming set and line up in columns.
- Let children choose the other words that rhyme.
- Have children pronounce the words.

## Transfer Words

- Tell children that they are going to use the rhyming words to spell some new words they might need when they are writing.
- Say the word and a sentence one of your children might write.
- Have children say the word and decide on the beginning letters.
- Write the beginning letters on an index card.
- Take the index card with the beginning letters to the pocket chart and have children say the columns of rhymes and the new word to find the rhyming pattern.
- Write the rhyming pattern on the card to finish the word.
- Have students write the word on paper or a whiteboard.

# Lesson 33

## kittens

**Letters:** e  i  k  n  s  t  t  (The vowel sounds for **i** and **e** are reviewed.)

**Make:** it  kit  sit  set  net  ten  Ken  nest  test  tent  kitten  kittens

**Sort:**

| it | set | Ken | nest |
|----|-----|-----|------|
| kit | net | ten | test |
| sit | | | |

**Transfer:** jet  west  chest

## Make Words

- Have children name and hold up letters.
- Tell children how many letters to use to make each word.
- Have children say each word and stretch out some words.
- Give sentences to clarify meaning.
- Give specific instructions on how to change words:
  — Add one letter.
  — Change the first letter.
  — Use the same letters.
- Have children clear their holders before making an unrelated word.
- Make sure children use a capital **K** when spelling the name **Ken**.
- Have children correct their word once it is made in the pocket chart.
- Give children one minute to figure out the secret word and then give them clues.

## Sort Words

- Put words in pocket chart in the order made.
- Have children say and spell each word.
- Remind them of how each word was changed to spell the new word.
- Select one word from each rhyming set and line up in columns.
- Let children choose the other words that rhyme.
- Have children pronounce the words.

## Transfer Words

- Tell children that they are going to use the rhyming words to spell some new words they might need when they are writing.
- Say the word and a sentence one of your children might write.
- Have children say the word and decide on the beginning letters.
- Write the beginning letters on an index card.
- Take the index card with the beginning letters to the pocket chart and have children say the columns of rhymes and the new word to find the rhyming pattern.
- Write the rhyming pattern on the card to finish the word.
- Have students write the word on paper or a whiteboard.

# Lesson 34

## mittens

**Letters:** | e | i | m | n | s | t | t |  (The vowel sounds for **i** and **e** are reviewed.)

**Make:** in  it  sit  set  met  men  ten  tin  tint  tent  sent  mittens

**Sort:**

| met | it | men | tent |
|-----|-----|-----|------|
| set | sit | ten | sent |

**Transfer:** wet   spent   jet

## Make Words

- Have children name and hold up letters.
- Tell children how many letters to use to make each word.
- Have children say each word and stretch out some words.
- Give sentences to clarify meaning.
- Give specific instructions on how to change words:
    — Add one letter.
    — Change the first letter.
    — Use the same letters.
- Have children clear their holders before making an unrelated word.
- Have children correct their word once it is made in the pocket chart.
- Give children one minute to figure out the secret word and then give them clues.

## Sort Words

- Put words in pocket chart in the order made.
- Have children say and spell each word.
- Remind them of how each word was changed to spell the new word.
- Select one word from each rhyming set and line up in columns.
- Let children choose the other words that rhyme.
- Have children pronounce the words.

## Transfer Words

- Tell children that they are going to use the rhyming words to spell some new words they might need when they are writing.
- Say the word and a sentence one of your children might write.
- Have children say the word and decide on the beginning letters.
- Write the beginning letters on an index card.
- Take the index card with the beginning letters to the pocket chart and have children say the columns of rhymes and the new word to find the rhyming pattern.
- Write the rhyming pattern on the card to finish the word.
- Have students write the word on paper or a whiteboard.

# Lesson 35

## lipstick

**Letters:**  i  i  c  k  l  p  s  t   (The vowel sound for **i** is reviewed.)

**Make:** sit  pit  tip  lip  clip  slip  lips  lick  pick  sick  stick  lipstick

**Sort:**

| pick | pit | tip |
|------|-----|-----|
| sick | sit | lip |
| lick |     | clip |
| stick |    | slip |

**Transfer:** brick    ship    thick

## Make Words

- Have children name and hold up letters.
- Tell children how many letters to use to make each word.
- Have children say each word and stretch out some words.
- Give sentences to clarify meaning.
- Give specific instructions on how to change words:
  — Add one letter.
  — Change the first letter.
  — Use the same letters.
- Have children clear their holders before making an unrelated word.
- Have children correct their word once it is made in the pocket chart.
- Give children one minute to figure out the secret word and then give them clues.

## Sort Words

- Put words in pocket chart in the order made.
- Have children say and spell each word.
- Remind them of how each word was changed to spell the new word.
- Select one word from each rhyming set and line up in columns.
- Let children choose the other words that rhyme.
- Have children pronounce the words.

## Transfer Words

- Tell children that they are going to use the rhyming words to spell some new words they might need when they are writing.
- Say the word and a sentence one of your children might write.
- Have children say the word and decide on the beginning letters.
- Write the beginning letters on an index card.
- Take the index card with the beginning letters to the pocket chart and have children say the columns of rhymes and the new word to find the rhyming pattern.
- Write the rhyming pattern on the card to finish the word.
- Have students write the word on paper or a whiteboard.

# Lesson 36

## blanket

**Letters:** | a | e | b | k | l | n | t | (The vowel sounds for **a** and **e** are reviewed.)

**Make:** bat  bet  net  Nat  tan  ten  Ken  Ben  ban  bank
blank  blanket

**Sort:**

| bat | net | tan | bank | Ben |
|-----|-----|-----|------|-----|
| Nat | bet | ban | blank | Ken |

**Transfer:** thank  plan  wet

## Make Words

- Have children name and hold up letters.
- Tell children how many letters to use to make each word.
- Have children say each word and stretch out some words.
- Give sentences to clarify meaning.
- Give specific instructions on how to change words:
  — Add one letter.
  — Change the first letter.
  — Use the same letters.
- Have children clear their holders before making an unrelated word.
- Make sure children use a capital letter when spelling the names **Nat**, **Ken**, and **Ben**.
- Have children correct their word once it is made in the pocket chart.
- Give children one minute to figure out the secret word and then give them clues.

## Sort Words

- Put words in pocket chart in the order made.
- Have children say and spell each word.
- Remind them of how each word was changed to spell the new word.
- Select one word from each rhyming set and line up in columns.
- Let children choose the other words that rhyme.
- Have children pronounce the words.

## Transfer Words

- Tell children that they are going to use the rhyming words to spell some new words they might need when they are writing.
- Say the word and a sentence one of your children might write.
- Have children say the word and decide on the beginning letters.
- Write the beginning letters on an index card.
- Take the index card with the beginning letters to the pocket chart and have children say the columns of rhymes and the new word to find the rhyming pattern.
- Write the rhyming pattern on the card to finish the word.
- Have students write the word on paper or a whiteboard.

# Lesson 37
## plastic

**Letters:** a  i  c  l  p  s  t   (The vowel sounds for **a** and **i** are reviewed.)

**Make:**   sit  sat  lip  lap  clap  clip  slip  last  list  slit  split  plastic

**Sort:**

| | | |
|---|---|---|
| lip | clap | slit |
| clip | lap | split |
| slip | | sit |

**Transfer:**   ship   strap   it

## Make Words

- Have children name and hold up letters.
- Tell children how many letters to use to make each word.
- Have children say each word and stretch out some words.
- Give sentences to clarify meaning.
- Give specific instructions on how to change words:
  — Add one letter.
  — Change the first letter.
  — Use the same letters.
- Have children clear their holders before making an unrelated word.
- Have children correct their word once it is made in the pocket chart.
- Give children one minute to figure out the secret word and then give them clues.

## Sort Words

- Put words in pocket chart in the order made.
- Have children say and spell each word.
- Remind them of how each word was changed to spell the new word.
- Select one word from each rhyming set and line up in columns.
- Let children choose the other words that rhyme.
- Have children pronounce the words.

## Transfer Words

- Tell children that they are going to use the rhyming words to spell some new words they might need when they are writing.
- Say the word and a sentence one of your children might write.
- Have children say the word and decide on the beginning letters.
- Write the beginning letters on an index card.
- Take the index card with the beginning letters to the pocket chart and have children say the columns of rhymes and the new word to find the rhyming pattern.
- Write the rhyming pattern on the card to finish the word.
- Have students write the word on paper or a whiteboard.

# Lesson 38

## bathtub

**Letters:** | a | u | b | b | h | t | t |  (The vowel sounds for **a** and **u** are reviewed.)

**Make:**  at  hat  hut  but  bat  tab  tub  hub  bath  bathtub

**Sort:**

| but | hat | tub |
|-----|-----|-----|
| hut | at  | hub |
|     | bat |     |

**Transfer:**  rub  flat  shut

## Make Words

- Have children name and hold up letters.
- Tell children how many letters to use to make each word.
- Have children say each word and stretch out some words.
- Give sentences to clarify meaning.
- Give specific instructions on how to change words:
  — Add one letter.
  — Change the first letter.
  — Use the same letters.
- Have children clear their holders before making an unrelated word.
- Have children correct their word once it is made in the pocket chart.
- Give children one minute to figure out the secret word and then give them clues.

## Sort Words

- Put words in pocket chart in the order made.
- Have children say and spell each word.
- Remind them of how each word was changed to spell the new word.
- Select one word from each rhyming set and line up in columns.
- Let children choose the other words that rhyme.
- Have children pronounce the words.

## Transfer Words

- Tell children that they are going to use the rhyming words to spell some new words they might need when they are writing.
- Say the word and a sentence one of your children might write.
- Have children say the word and decide on the beginning letters.
- Write the beginning letters on an index card.
- Take the index card with the beginning letters to the pocket chart and have children say the columns of rhymes and the new word to find the rhyming pattern.
- Write the rhyming pattern on the card to finish the word.
- Have students write the word on paper or a whiteboard.

# Lesson 39

## shopping

**Letters:** | i | o | g | h | n | p | p | s |  (The vowel sounds for **i** and **o** are reviewed.)

**Make:** on   in   pin   nip   hip   hop   shop   ship   sing   song
hopping   shopping

**Sort:**

| nip | shop | in | hopping |
|-----|------|-----|---------|
| hip | hop | pin | shopping |
| ship | | | |

**Transfer:** chin      chop      chopping

## Make Words

- Have children name and hold up letters.
- Tell children how many letters to use to make each word.
- Have children say each word and stretch out some words.
- Give sentences to clarify meaning.
- Give specific instructions on how to change words:
  — Add one letter.
  — Change the first letter.
  — Use the same letters.
- Have children clear their holders before making an unrelated word.
- Have children correct their word once it is made in the pocket chart.
- Give children one minute to figure out the secret word and then give them clues.

## Sort Words

- Put words in pocket chart in the order made.
- Have children say and spell each word.
- Remind them of how each word was changed to spell the new word.
- Select one word from each rhyming set and line up in columns.
- Let children choose the other words that rhyme.
- Have children pronounce the words.

## Transfer Words

- Tell children that they are going to use the rhyming words to spell some new words they might need when they are writing.
- Say the word and a sentence one of your children might write.
- Have children say the word and decide on the beginning letters.
- Write the beginning letters on an index card.
- Take the index card with the beginning letters to the pocket chart and have children say the columns of rhymes and the new word to find the rhyming pattern.
- Write the rhyming pattern on the card to finish the word.
- Have students write the word on paper or a whiteboard.

# Lesson 40

## stocking

**Letters:** | i | o | c | g | k | n | s | t |  (The vowels sounds for **i** and **o** are reviewed.)

**Make:** ink  pink  sink  sing  king  sick  sock  stock  stick
sting  stink  stocking

**Sort:**
| sink | sink | sick | sock |
| pink | king | stick | stock |
| ink | sting | | |
| stink | | | |

**Transfer:** wink  thick  shock

## Make Words

- Have children name and hold up letters.
- Tell children how many letters to use to make each word.
- Have children say each word and stretch out some words.
- Give sentences to clarify meaning.
- Give specific instructions on how to change words:
  — Add one letter.
  — Change the first letter.
  — Use the same letters.
- Have children clear their holders before making an unrelated word.
- Have children correct their word once it is made in the pocket chart.
- Give children one minute to figure out the secret word and then give them clues.

## Sort Words

- Put words in pocket chart in the order made.
- Have children say and spell each word.
- Remind them of how each word was changed to spell the new word.
- Select one word from each rhyming set and line up in columns.
- Let children choose the other words that rhyme.
- Have children pronounce the words.

## Transfer Words

- Tell children that they are going to use the rhyming words to spell some new words they might need when they are writing.
- Say the word and a sentence one of your children might write.
- Have children say the word and decide on the beginning letters.
- Write the beginning letters on an index card.
- Take the index card with the beginning letters to the pocket chart and have children say the columns of rhymes and the new word to find the rhyming pattern.
- Write the rhyming pattern on the card to finish the word.
- Have students write the word on paper or a whiteboard.

# Assessment Lessons 31-40

In these lessons, you will **assess the consonants j, k, and w and the common sound for the vowels.** Some children may have trouble telling you the vowel sound but words with these vowels will continue to be made throughout the lessons. Continue to assess children for any sound not yet mastered at each assessment point. (No new items for segmenting and blending were added. You may want to reassess any students who have not demonstrated on previous assessments that they have these skills.)

| Letter | Name | Sound | Word | Segments | | Blends | |
|--------|------|-------|------|----------|---|--------|---|
| **After Lesson 10** | | | | | | | |
| a | | | | sat | | ran | |
| d | | | | band | | last | |
| n | | | | ant | | and | |
| s | | | | rat | | rag | |
| b | | | | past | | trap | |
| t | | | | | | | |
| l | | | | | | | |
| r | | | | | | | |
| p | | | | | | | |
| **After Lesson 20** | | | | | | | |
| c | | | | nut | | tug | |
| f | | | | hunt | | send | |
| g | | | | pet | | pest | |
| h | | | | pin | | trip | |
| m | | | | spot | | mop | |
| **After Lesson 30** | | | | | | | |
| sh | | | | ship | | chip | |
| ch | | | | mash | | cash | |
| th | | | | than | | thin | |
| **After Lesson 40** | | | | | | | |
| j | | | | | | | |
| k | | | | | | | |
| w | | | | | | | |
| a | | | | | | | |
| e | | | | | | | |
| i | | | | | | | |
| o | | | | | | | |
| u | | | | | | | |

# Lessons 41-50

In these lessons, students have only one vowel but that vowel is often followed by an **r**. Students learn to decode and spell words with **ar**, **ir**, **or**, and **ur**.

## Lesson 41
### smart

**Letters:** **a**, **m**, **r**, **s**, **t**   (Rhyming pattern **art**)

**Words to Make:** **am**   **at**   **art**   **arm**   **ram**   **rat**   **mat**   **mart**   **Mars**   **star**   **smart**

## Part One • Making Words

Have the children arrange their letters in front of their holders to match the pocket-chart letters, with the vowel first and the other letters in alphabetical order.

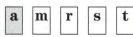

Begin the lesson by naming each pocket-chart letter. Have children hold up their little letter cards as you hold up the large letter cards.

**am**   "The first word we are going to spell is **am**. I **am** your teacher. Everyone say **am**. Use 2 letters to spell **am**."

Choose a child who has **am** spelled correctly to spell **am** with the pocket-chart letters. Have the class chorally spell **am** and fix their word if **am** is not correct.

**at**   "The next word we are going to spell is **at**. We are **at** school. Everyone say **at**. Change the last letter to spell **at**."

Let a child who has **at** spelled correctly spell **at** with the pocket-chart letters.

**art**   "Add a letter to **at** to spell **art**. We all like **art**. Everyone say **art**."

Continue the lesson, giving children explicit instruction about which letters to remove and where to add letters. Put each word in a sentence and have children say each word before making it. Have them "stretch" some words to provide practice for children who are still learning to segment words. Let a child who has spelled the word correctly come to the front of the room and make that word with the pocket-chart letters. Choose

your struggling readers when the word is an easy word and choose your advanced readers for harder words. Have the children chorally spell each word after it is made in the pocket chart and fix their word to match.

| | |
|---|---|
| **arm** | "Change the last letter in **art** to spell **arm**. Here is my **arm**. Everyone say **arm**." |
| **ram** | "Move the letter in **arm** to spell **ram**. Some teams have a **ram** as their mascot. Everyone say **ram**." |
| **rat** | "Change the last letter to spell **rat**. A **rat** likes to eat cheese. Everyone say **rat**." |
| **mat** | "Change the first letter to spell **mat**. Did you nap on your **mat** in kindergarten? Everyone say **mat**." |
| **mart** | "Add 1 letter to **mat** to spell **mart**. Do you shop at **Kmart** or **Wal-Mart**? Everyone say **mart**." |
| **Mars** | "Change the last letter to spell **Mars**. **Mars** is the name of one of the planets. Everyone say **Mars**. Remember that **Mars** is the **name** of a planet." |
| **star** | "Clear your holders and start over to spell **star**. I saw a bright **star** in the sky. Everyone say **star**. Use 4 letters to spell **star**." |
| **smart** | **(the secret word)** "We have one more word to spell. It is the word that uses all the letters—the secret word. Move your letters in your holder and see if you can figure out the secret word. Signal me if you think you have it." |

If no one makes the secret word in one minute, give them a clue.

"Our secret word starts with **s-m** and is what you all are."

End the making words part of the lesson by having one child spell **smart** in the pocket chart and letting everyone hold up their holders to show you **smart** made in their holders. Have them close the holders and turn their attention to the pocket chart.

# Part Two • Sorting Words (Sort for **am**, **at**, and **art**)

Tell your students that they are going to say all the words they spelled and then sort the rhyming words. Using the index cards with the words, place them in the pocket chart and have the children pronounce them. Remind the children of what they changed to make each word.

"First we used 2 letters to spell **am**, **a-m**."

"We changed the **m** to a **t** to spell **at**, **a-t**."

"We added an **r** to **at** to spell **art**, **a-r-t**."

"We changed the last letter and spelled **arm**, **a-r-m**."

"We moved the letters in **arm** around to spell **ram**, **r-a-m**."

"We changed the **m** to a **t** to spell **rat**, **r-a-t**."

"We changed the first letter to spell **mat**, **m-a-t**."

"We added the **r** to change mat to **mart**, **m-a-r-t**."

"We changed the first letter and used a capital **M** to spell **Mars**, **M-a-r-s**."

"We started over and used 4 letters to spell **star**, **s-t-a-r**."

"Our secret word today was what you all are—**smart**, **s-m-a-r-t**."

"Now we need to sort out the rhymes. I will take one of each set and you can come and help me find the others."

Arrange one of each set of rhyming words to begin three columns.

**am**  **smart**  **rat**

Choose three children and help them choose the rhyming words and line them up in columns. Have the rhyming words pronounced and have children notice that they all rhyme and they all have the same letters from the vowel to the end of the word.

| am | smart | rat |
|----|-------|-----|
| ram | art | at |
| | mart | mat |

# Part Three • Transfer  jam  start  clam

Have the children take out paper. Tell them that you are going to say a word that someone might be writing. By figuring out the rhyming pattern, they will be able to spell the word.

"The first word we are going to spell is **jam**. Robert might be writing that he likes strawberry **jam**. Let's all say **jam** and listen for the beginning letter."

Write **j** on an index card when the children decide that **jam** begins with **j**. Take the index card to the pocket chart and have the children pronounce **jam** with each set of rhyming words. When they decide that **jam** rhymes with **am** and **ram**, write **a-m** next to **j**. Have children write **jam** on their papers.

Repeat this procedure for **start** and **clam**.

# Lesson 42

## charm

Letters: | a | c | h | m | r |  (Rhyming patterns **arm**, **arch**)

**Make:**  am   arm   ram   car   ham   harm   arch   march   charm

**Sort:**

| am | charm | arch |
|------|-------|-------|
| ram | arm | march |
| ham | harm | |

**Transfer:**  farm       Pam       swam

## Make Words

- Have children name and hold up letters.
- Tell children how many letters to use to make each word.
- Have children say each word and stretch out some words.
- Give sentences to clarify meaning.
- Give specific instructions on how to change words:
  — Add one letter.
  — Change the first letter.
  — Use the same letters.
- Have children clear their holders before making an unrelated word.
- Have children correct their word once it is made in the pocket chart.
- Give children one minute to figure out the secret word and then give them clues.

## Sort Words

- Put words in pocket chart in the order made.
- Have children say and spell each word.
- Remind them of how each word was changed to spell the new word.
- Select one word from each rhyming set and line up in columns.
- Let children choose the other words that rhyme.
- Have children pronounce the words.

## Transfer Words

- Tell children that they are going to use the rhyming words to spell some new words they might need when they are writing.
- Say the word and a sentence one of your children might write.
- Have children say the word and decide on the beginning letters.
- Write the beginning letters on an index card.
- Take the index card with the beginning letters to the pocket chart and have children say the columns of rhymes and the new word to find the rhyming pattern.
- Write the rhyming pattern on the card to finish the word.
- Have students write the word on paper or a whiteboard.

# Lesson 43

## chart

**Letters:** a c h r t (Rhyming patterns **ar**, **art**)

**Make:** at art tar car rat hat cat cart chart

**Sort:**

| | | |
|---|---|---|
| at | car | cart |
| cat | tar | chart |
| hat | | art |
| rat | | |

**Transfer:** smart star start

## Make Words

- Have children name and hold up letters.
- Tell children how many letters to use to make each word.
- Have children say each word and stretch out some words.
- Give sentences to clarify meaning.
- Give specific instructions on how to change words:
  — Add one letter.
  — Change the first letter.
  — Use the same letters.
- Have children clear their holders before making an unrelated word.
- Have children correct their word once it is made in the pocket chart.
- Give children one minute to figure out the secret word and then give them clues.

## Sort Words

- Put words in pocket chart in the order made.
- Have children say and spell each word.
- Remind them of how each word was changed to spell the new word.
- Select one word from each rhyming set and line up in columns.
- Let children choose the other words that rhyme.
- Have children pronounce the words.

## Transfer Words

- Tell children that they are going to use the rhyming words to spell some new words they might need when they are writing.
- Say the word and a sentence one of your children might write.
- Have children say the word and decide on the beginning letters.
- Write the beginning letters on an index card.
- Take the index card with the beginning letters to the pocket chart and have children say the columns of rhymes and the new word to find the rhyming pattern.
- Write the rhyming pattern on the card to finish the word.
- Have students write the word on paper or a whiteboard.

# Lesson 44
## first

**Letters:** | i | f | r | s | t |   (Rhyming patterns **ir**, **it**)

**Make:**   if   is   it   fit   sit   sir   stir   sift   fist   first

**Sort:**
| sir  | it  |
|------|-----|
| stir | sit |

**Transfer:**   bit        spit        split

## Make Words

- Have children name and hold up letters.
- Tell children how many letters to use to make each word.
- Have children say each word and stretch out some words.
- Give sentences to clarify meaning.
- Give specific instructions on how to change words:
  — Add one letter.
  — Change the first letter.
  — Use the same letters.
- Have children clear their holders before making an unrelated word.
- Have children correct their word once it is made in the pocket chart.
- Give children one minute to figure out the secret word and then give them clues.

## Sort Words

- Put words in pocket chart in the order made.
- Have children say and spell each word.
- Remind them of how each word was changed to spell the new word.
- Select one word from each rhyming set and line up in columns.
- Let children choose the other words that rhyme.
- Have children pronounce the words.

## Transfer Words

- Tell children that they are going to use the rhyming words to spell some new words they might need when they are writing.
- Say the word and a sentence one of your children might write.
- Have children say the word and decide on the beginning letters.
- Write the beginning letters on an index card.
- Take the index card with the beginning letters to the pocket chart and have children say the columns of rhymes and the new word to find the rhyming pattern.
- Write the rhyming pattern on the card to finish the word.
- Have students write the word on paper or a whiteboard.

# Lesson 45

## squirt

**Letters:** i u q r s t (The **qu** combination is introduced.)

**Make:** is  it  sit  sir  stir  rust  ruts  quit  quits  squirt

**Sort:**
| | |
|---|---|
| it | sir |
| sit | stir |
| quit | |

**Transfer:** fit  hit  grit

## Make Words

- Have children name and hold up letters.
- Tell children how many letters to use to make each word.
- Have children say each word and stretch out some words.
- Give sentences to clarify meaning.
- Give specific instructions on how to change words:
  — Add one letter.
  — Change the first letter.
  — Use the same letters.
- Have children clear their holders before making an unrelated word.
- Have children correct their word once it is made in the pocket chart.
- Give children one minute to figure out the secret word and then give them clues.

## Sort Words

- Put words in pocket chart in the order made.
- Have children say and spell each word.
- Remind them of how each word was changed to spell the new word.
- Select one word from each rhyming set and line up in columns.
- Let children choose the other words that rhyme.
- Have children pronounce the words.

## Transfer Words

- Tell children that they are going to use the rhyming words to spell some new words they might need when they are writing.
- Say the word and a sentence one of your children might write.
- Have children say the word and decide on the beginning letters.
- Write the beginning letters on an index card.
- Take the index card with the beginning letters to the pocket chart and have children say the columns of rhymes and the new word to find the rhyming pattern.
- Write the rhyming pattern on the card to finish the word.
- Have students write the word on paper or a whiteboard.

# Lesson 46

## string

**Letters:** | i | g | n | r | s | t |  (Rhyming patterns **ing, it, ir, in**)

**Make:**    it    in    tin    sit    sir    stir    grin    ring    sing    sting    string

**Sort:**

| sing | it | sir | in |
|------|-----|------|-----|
| ring | sit | stir | tin |
| sting | | | grin |
| string | | | |

**Transfer:**    wing      king      thin

## Make Words

- Have children name and hold up letters.
- Tell children how many letters to use to make each word.
- Have children say each word and stretch out some words.
- Give sentences to clarify meaning.
- Give specific instructions on how to change words:
  — Add one letter.
  — Change the first letter.
  — Use the same letters.
- Have children clear their holders before making an unrelated word.
- Have children correct their word once it is made in the pocket chart.
- Give children one minute to figure out the secret word and then give them clues.

## Sort Words

- Put words in pocket chart in the order made.
- Have children say and spell each word.
- Remind them of how each word was changed to spell the new word.
- Select one word from each rhyming set and line up in columns.
- Let children choose the other words that rhyme.
- Have children pronounce the words.

## Transfer Words

- Tell children that they are going to use the rhyming words to spell some new words they might need when they are writing.
- Say the word and a sentence one of your children might write.
- Have children say the word and decide on the beginning letters.
- Write the beginning letters on an index card.
- Take the index card with the beginning letters to the pocket chart and have children say the columns of rhymes and the new word to find the rhyming pattern.
- Write the rhyming pattern on the card to finish the word.
- Have students write the word on paper or a whiteboard.

# Lesson 47

## popcorn

**Letters:** | o | o | c | n | p | p | r |  (Rhyming patterns **op**, **on**)

**Make:**  or  on  con  pop  cop  crop  prop  corn  popcorn

**Sort:**

| cop | on |
|------|------|
| crop | con |
| prop | |
| pop | |

**Transfer:**  hop  crop  shop

## Make Words

- Have children name and hold up letters.
- Tell children how many letters to use to make each word.
- Have children say each word and stretch out some words.
- Give sentences to clarify meaning.
- Give specific instructions on how to change words:
  — Add one letter.
  — Change the first letter.
  — Use the same letters.
- Have children clear their holders before making an unrelated word.
- Have children correct their word once it is made in the pocket chart.
- Give children one minute to figure out the secret word and then give them clues.

## Sort Words

- Put words in pocket chart in the order made.
- Have children say and spell each word.
- Remind them of how each word was changed to spell the new word.
- Select one word from each rhyming set and line up in columns.
- Let children choose the other words that rhyme.
- Have children pronounce the words.

## Transfer Words

- Tell children that they are going to use the rhyming words to spell some new words they might need when they are writing.
- Say the word and a sentence one of your children might write.
- Have children say the word and decide on the beginning letters.
- Write the beginning letters on an index card.
- Take the index card with the beginning letters to the pocket chart and have children say the columns of rhymes and the new word to find the rhyming pattern.
- Write the rhyming pattern on the card to finish the word.
- Have students write the word on paper or a whiteboard.

# Lesson 48

## visitors

**Letters:** `i` `i` `o` `r` `s` `t` `v`   (The letter **v** is introduced.)

**Make:**  or   is   it   sit   sir   stir   sort   rots   visit   visitor

**Sort:**   sir        it
            stir       sit

**Transfer:**  bit         fit         split

## Make Words

- Have children name and hold up letters.
- Tell children how many letters to use to make each word.
- Have children say each word and stretch out some words.
- Give sentences to clarify meaning.
- Give specific instructions on how to change words:
  — Add one letter.
  — Change the first letter.
  — Use the same letters.
- Have children clear their holders before making an unrelated word.
- Have children correct their word once it is made in the pocket chart.
- Give children one minute to figure out the secret word and then give them clues.

## Sort Words

- Put words in pocket chart in the order made.
- Have children say and spell each word.
- Remind them of how each word was changed to spell the new word.
- Select one word from each rhyming set and line up in columns.
- Let children choose the other words that rhyme.
- Have children pronounce the words.

## Transfer Words

- Tell children that they are going to use the rhyming words to spell some new words they might need when they are writing.
- Say the word and a sentence one of your children might write.
- Have children say the word and decide on the beginning letters.
- Write the beginning letters on an index card.
- Take the index card with the beginning letters to the pocket chart and have children say the columns of rhymes and the new word to find the rhyming pattern.
- Write the rhyming pattern on the card to finish the word.
- Have students write the word on paper or a whiteboard.

# Lesson 49

## burst

**Letters:** u  b  r  s  t   (Rhyming patterns **ub**, **us**, **ut**, **ust**)

**Make:**  us  bus  but  rut  rub  sub  tub  tubs  stub  rust  bust  burst

**Sort:**

| rub | us | but | rust |
|-----|-----|-----|------|
| tub | bus | rut | bust |
| sub | | | |
| stub | | | |

**Transfer:**  just  club  must

## Make Words

- Have children name and hold up letters.
- Tell children how many letters to use to make each word.
- Have children say each word and stretch out some words.
- Give sentences to clarify meaning.
- Give specific instructions on how to change words:
  — Add one letter.
  — Change the first letter.
  — Use the same letters.
- Have children clear their holders before making an unrelated word.
- Have children correct their word once it is made in the pocket chart.
- Give children one minute to figure out the secret word and then give them clues.

## Sort Words

- Put words in pocket chart in the order made.
- Have children say and spell each word.
- Remind them of how each word was changed to spell the new word.
- Select one word from each rhyming set and line up in columns.
- Let children choose the other words that rhyme.
- Have children pronounce the words.

## Transfer Words

- Tell children that they are going to use the rhyming words to spell some new words they might need when they are writing.
- Say the word and a sentence one of your children might write.
- Have children say the word and decide on the beginning letters.
- Write the beginning letters on an index card.
- Take the index card with the beginning letters to the pocket chart and have children say the columns of rhymes and the new word to find the rhyming pattern.
- Write the rhyming pattern on the card to finish the word.
- Have students write the word on paper or a whiteboard.

# Lesson 50
## hunting

**Letters:**  | i | u | g | h | n | r | t |  (Rhyming patterns **it, ut, ug, unt**)

**Make:**  it  hit  hut  rut  rug  hug  hurt  hunt  runt  turn  grunt  hurting

**Sort:**

| it | rug | hut | runt |
|----|-----|-----|------|
| hit | hug | rut | hunt |
| | | | grunt |

**Transfer:**  bug  jug  stunt

## Make Words

- Have children name and hold up letters.
- Tell children how many letters to use to make each word.
- Have children say each word and stretch out some words.
- Give sentences to clarify meaning.
- Give specific instructions on how to change words:
  — Add one letter.
  — Change the first letter.
  — Use the same letters.
- Have children clear their holders before making an unrelated word.
- Have children correct their word once it is made in the pocket chart.
- Give children one minute to figure out the secret word and then give them clues.

## Sort Words

- Put words in pocket chart in the order made.
- Have children say and spell each word.
- Remind them of how each word was changed to spell the new word.
- Select one word from each rhyming set and line up in columns.
- Let children choose the other words that rhyme.
- Have children pronounce the words.

## Transfer Words

- Tell children that they are going to use the rhyming words to spell some new words they might need when they are writing.
- Say the word and a sentence one of your children might write.
- Have children say the word and decide on the beginning letters.
- Write the beginning letters on an index card.
- Take the index card with the beginning letters to the pocket chart and have children say the columns of rhymes and the new word to find the rhyming pattern.
- Write the rhyming pattern on the card to finish the word.
- Have students write the word on paper or a whiteboard.

**In this and all remaining assessments, you will assess your students' ability to spell words that rhyme with other words.** You can do these assessments with your whole class but be sure children are writing the word by themselves and cannot see what anyone else is writing. You may want to begin a new record sheet to record the children's progress in the remaining lessons. For each word, record by checking if the child used the correct rhyming pattern and the correct beginning letters. If students did not use the correct pattern or beginning letters, record what they did use and analyze their errors.

For this first assessment, we will use rhyming sets that are quite different from one another. They all have different vowels and different ending letters. In later assessments, the words will be more similar.

Tell the children to pretend they are writing a story and need to spell some words. To spell a word they should stretch out the word and write the beginning letters and then decide which rhyming words will help them finish the word. Be sure that your students understand that this is exactly what they do in the transfer step of each Making Words lesson but now you want to see if they can do it on their own.

Write these words in columns and have your children chorally pronounce and spell them. Have them notice that each column of words has the same letters from the vowel to the end of the words and that the words in the column rhyme.

| at | in | hop |
|------|------|------|
| hat | pin | pop |
| bat | win | top |

Have the children number a sheet of paper from 1 to 5. Say a word and put it in a sentence. Ask your students to stretch out each word to hear the beginning letters and then decide which words it rhymes with to finish spelling the word:

     **mop**      **tin**      **flat**      **chin**      **shop**

Here is one child's record sheet marked with 2 errors.

Child's Name _____

| Word | Beginning Letters | Rhyming Pattern |
|------|------|------|
| **After Lesson 50** | | |
| mop | m | op |
| tin | t | in |
| flat | fl | at |
| chin | ch | in |
| shop | sh | op |
| | | |

Child's Name ___Cooper H___

| Word | Beginning Letters | Rhyming Pattern |
|------|------|------|
| **After Lesson 50** | 2/16 | 2/16 |
| mop | m ✓ | op *ap* |
| tin | t ✓ | in ✓ |
| flat | fl ✓ | at ✓ |
| chin | ch *sh* | in ✓ |
| shop | sh ✓ | op ✓ |
| | | |

# Lessons 51-60

These 10 lessons introduce the vowel pairs **ee**, **ea**, and **oa** and the consonant **x**.

## Lesson 51

### sixteen

**Letters:** e, e, i, n, s, t, x   (The vowel combination **ee** is introduced.)

**Words to Make:** it  sit  six  net  set  see  seen  teen  next  exit  sixteen

## Part One • Making Words

Have the children arrange their letters in front of their holders to match the pocket-chart letters, with the vowels first and the other letters in alphabetical order.

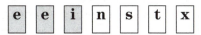

Ask the children to hold up and name each letter and then begin making words.

**it**    "The first word we are going to spell is **it**. **It** is a rainy day. Everyone say **it**. Use 2 letters to spell **it**."

Choose a child who has **it** spelled correctly to spell **it** with the pocket-chart letters. Have the class chorally spell **it** and fix their word if **it** is not correct.

**sit**   "Add 1 letter to spell **sit**. Please **sit** down. Everyone say **sit**."

Let a child who has **sit** spelled correctly spell **sit** with the pocket-chart letters.

**six**   "Change the last letter to spell **six**. Raise your hand if you are **six** years old. Everyone say **six**."

Continue the lesson, giving children explicit instruction about which letters to remove and where to add letters. Put each word in a sentence and have children say each word before making it. Have them "stretch" some words to provide practice for children who are still learning to segment words. Let a child who has spelled the word correctly come to the front of the room and make that word with the pocket-chart letters. Choose

your struggling readers when the word is an easy word and choose your advanced readers for harder words. Have the children chorally spell each word after it is made in the pocket chart and fix their word to match.

**net** "Clear your holders and use 3 letters to spell **net**. In tennis, you have to hit the ball over the **net**. Everyone say **net**."

**set** "Change the first letter to spell **set**. Please **set** the table. Everyone say **set**."

**see** "Change the last letter to spell **see**. I **see** you all working hard. Everyone say **see**."

**seen** Add a letter to spell **seen**. Has anyone **seen** the movie *Cinderella*? Everyone say **seen**."

**teen** "Change the first letter to spell **teen**. When you turn 13, you are a **teen**. Everyone say **teen**."

**nest** "Clear your holders and use 4 letters to spell **nest**. The birds were building a **nest**. Everyone say **nest**."

**next** "Change just 1 letter to turn **nest** into **next**. Who likes to sit **next** to their friend on the bus? Everyone say **next**."

**exit** "Clear your holders and start over to spell **exit**. You go out through the **exit**. Everyone say **exit**. Use 4 letters to spell **exit**."

**sixteen** **(the secret word)** "We have one more word to spell. It is the word that uses all the letters—the secret word. Move your letters in your holder and see if you can figure out the secret word. Signal me if you think you have it."

If no one makes the secret word in one minute, give them a clue.

"Our secret word combines 2 words you already spelled."

End the making words part of the lesson by having one child spell **sixteen** in the pocket chart and letting everyone hold up their holders to show you **sixteen** made in their holders. Have them close the holders and turn their attention to the pocket chart.

# Part Two • Sorting Words (The patterns **it**, **et**, and **een**)

Tell your students that they are going to say all the words they spelled and then sort the rhyming words. Using the index cards with the words, place them in the pocket chart and have the children pronounce them. Remind the children of what they changed to make each word.

"First we used 2 letters to spell **it**, **i-t**."

"We added an **s** to spell **sit**, **s-i-t**."

"We changed the last letter to an **x** to spell **six**, **s-i-x**."

"We started over and used 3 letters to spell **net**, **n-e-t**."

"We changed the first letter to spell **set**, **s-e-t**."

"We changed the last letter to spell **see, s-e-e**."

"We added a letter to spell **seen, s-e-e-n**."

"We changed the first letter to spell **teen, t-e-e-n**."

"We started over and used 4 letters to spell **nest, n-e-s-t**."

"We changed the **s** to an **x** to spell **next, n-e-x-t**."

"We started over and used 4 letters to spell **exit, e-x-i-t**."

"Our secret word today was **sixteen, s-i-x-t-e-e-n**."

"Now we need to sort out the rhymes. I will take one of each set and you can come and help me find the others."

Arrange one of each set of rhyming words to begin three columns.

**sit**      **set**      **seen**

Choose three children and help them choose the rhyming words and line them up in columns. Have the rhyming words pronounced and have children notice that they all rhyme and they all have the same letters from the vowel to the end of the word.

**sit**      **set**      **seen**

**it**       **net**      **teen**

# Part Three ● Transfer   vet   split   green

Have the children take out paper. Tell them that you are going to say a word that someone might be writing. By figuring out the rhyming pattern, they will be able to spell the word.

"The first word we are going to spell is **vet**. Rasheed might be writing about taking his dog to the **vet**. Let's all say **vet** and listen for the beginning letter."

Write **v** on an index card when the children decide that **vet** begins with **v**. Take the index card to the pocket chart and have the children pronounce **vet** with each set of rhyming words. When they decide that **vet** rhymes with **net** and **set**, write **et** next to **v**. Have the children write **vet** on their papers.

Repeat this procedure for **split** and **green**.

## speeding

**Letters:** [e] [e] [i] [d] [g] [n] [p] [s]  (Rhyming patterns **ed**, **eed**, **end**, **eep**)

**Make:** Ed  Ned  see  seed  need  deep  seep  send  spend  speed
seeing  speeding

**Sort:**

| Ed | seed | send | seep |
|---|---|---|---|
| Ned | need | spend | deep |
| | speed | | |

**Transfer:** bend  sheep  bleed

## Make Words

- Have children name and hold up letters.
- Tell children how many letters to use to make each word.
- Have children say each word and stretch out some words.
- Give sentences to clarify meaning.
- Give specific instructions on how to change words:
  — Add one letter.
  — Change the first letter.
  — Use the same letters.
- Have children clear their holders before making an unrelated word.
- Be sure children use capital letters when spelling names.
- Have children correct their word once it is made in the pocket chart.
- Give children one minute to figure out the secret word and then give them clues.

## Sort Words

- Put words in pocket chart in the order made.
- Have children say and spell each word.
- Remind them of how each word was changed to spell the new word.
- Select one word from each rhyming set and line up in columns.
- Let children choose the other words that rhyme.
- Have children pronounce the words.

## Transfer Words

- Tell children that they are going to use the rhyming words to spell some new words they might need when they are writing.
- Say the word and a sentence one of your children might write.
- Have children say the word and decide on the beginning letters.
- Write the beginning letters on an index card.
- Take the index card with the beginning letters to the pocket chart and have children say the columns of rhymes and the new word to find the rhyming pattern.
- Write the rhyming pattern on the card to finish the word.
- Have students write the word on paper or a whiteboard.

# Lesson 53

## shelter

**Letters:** | e | e | h | l | s | t | r | (Rhyming patterns **eet, ee, eel**)

**Make:** her  see  eel  heel  reel  steel  sleet  sheet  three  trees  shelter

**Sort:**

| | | |
|---|---|---|
| sleet | see | eel |
| sheet | three | heel |
| | | reel |
| | | steel |

**Transfer:** free     feel     street

## Make Words

- Have children name and hold up letters.
- Tell children how many letters to use to make each word.
- Have children say each word and stretch out some words.
- Give sentences to clarify meaning.
- Give specific instructions on how to change words:
  — Add one letter.
  — Change the first letter.
  — Use the same letters.
- Have children clear their holders before making an unrelated word.
- Have children correct their word once it is made in the pocket chart.
- Give children one minute to figure out the secret word and then give them clues.

## Sort Words

- Put words in pocket chart in the order made.
- Have children say and spell each word.
- Remind them of how each word was changed to spell the new word.
- Select one word from each rhyming set and line up in columns.
- Let children choose the other words that rhyme.
- Have children pronounce the words.

## Transfer Words

- Tell children that they are going to use the rhyming words to spell some new words they might need when they are writing.
- Say the word and a sentence one of your children might write.
- Have children say the word and decide on the beginning letters.
- Write the beginning letters on an index card.
- Take the index card with the beginning letters to the pocket chart and have children say the columns of rhymes and the new word to find the rhyming pattern.
- Write the rhyming pattern on the card to finish the word.
- Have students write the word on paper or a whiteboard.

# Lesson 54

## helpers

**Letters:** | e | e | h | l | p | r | s |  (Rhyming patterns **eel**, **eep**, **e**)

**Make:**    he   she   her   see   eel   heel   help   seep   sheep   sleep   helpers

**Sort:**

| eel | seep | he |
|------|-------|------|
| heel | sleep | she |
| | sheep | |

**Transfer:**   deep     keep     sweep

## Make Words

- Have children name and hold up letters.
- Tell children how many letters to use to make each word.
- Have children say each word and stretch out some words.
- Give sentences to clarify meaning.
- Give specific instructions on how to change words:
  — Add one letter.
  — Change the first letter.
  — Use the same letters.
- Have children clear their holders before making an unrelated word.
- Have children correct their word once it is made in the pocket chart.
- Give children one minute to figure out the secret word and then give them clues.

## Sort Words

- Put words in pocket chart in the order made.
- Have children say and spell each word.
- Remind them of how each word was changed to spell the new word.
- Select one word from each rhyming set and line up in columns.
- Let children choose the other words that rhyme.
- Have children pronounce the words.

## Transfer Words

- Tell children that they are going to use the rhyming words to spell some new words they might need when they are writing.
- Say the word and a sentence one of your children might write.
- Have children say the word and decide on the beginning letters.
- Write the beginning letters on an index card.
- Take the index card with the beginning letters to the pocket chart and have children say the columns of rhymes and the new word to find the rhyming pattern.
- Write the rhyming pattern on the card to finish the word.
- Have students write the word on paper or a whiteboard.

# Lesson 55

## stream

**Letters:** | a | e | m | r | s | t |  (Rhyming patterns **eat, ea, eam, et**)

**Make:** eat  tea  sea  met  set  seat  meat  team  east  stem
steam  stream

**Sort:**

| eat | sea | team | met |
|-----|-----|------|-----|
| seat | tea | steam | set |
| meat | | stream | |

**Transfer:** heat  cream  dream

## Make Words

- Have children name and hold up letters.
- Tell children how many letters to use to make each word.
- Have children say each word and stretch out some words.
- Give sentences to clarify meaning.
- Give specific instructions on how to change words:
  — Add one letter.
  — Change the first letter.
  — Use the same letters.
- Have children clear their holders before making an unrelated word.
- Have children correct their word once it is made in the pocket chart.
- Give children one minute to figure out the secret word and then give them clues.

## Sort Words

- Put words in pocket chart in the order made.
- Have children say and spell each word.
- Remind them of how each word was changed to spell the new word.
- Select one word from each rhyming set and line up in columns.
- Let children choose the other words that rhyme.
- Have children pronounce the words.

## Transfer Words

- Tell children that they are going to use the rhyming words to spell some new words they might need when they are writing.
- Say the word and a sentence one of your children might write.
- Have children say the word and decide on the beginning letters.
- Write the beginning letters on an index card.
- Take the index card with the beginning letters to the pocket chart and have children say the columns of rhymes and the new word to find the rhyming pattern.
- Write the rhyming pattern on the card to finish the word.
- Have students write the word on paper or a whiteboard.

# Lesson 56

## magnets

**Letters:** | a | e | g | m | n | s | t | (Rhyming patterns **eat**, **eam**, **et**)

**Make:** eat net met set seat neat meat team east stem
steam magnets

**Sort:**

| eat | team | net |
|------|-------|-----|
| seat | steam | met |
| neat | | set |

**Transfer:** stream treat wet

## Make Words

- Have children name and hold up letters.
- Tell children how many letters to use to make each word.
- Have children say each word and stretch out some words.
- Give sentences to clarify meaning.
- Give specific instructions on how to change words:
  — Add one letter.
  — Change the first letter.
  — Use the same letters.
- Have children clear their holders before making an unrelated word.
- Have children correct their word once it is made in the pocket chart.
- Give children one minute to figure out the secret word and then give them clues.

## Sort Words

- Put words in pocket chart in the order made.
- Have children say and spell each word.
- Remind them of how each word was changed to spell the new word.
- Select one word from each rhyming set and line up in columns.
- Let children choose the other words that rhyme.
- Have children pronounce the words.

## Transfer Words

- Tell children that they are going to use the rhyming words to spell some new words they might need when they are writing.
- Say the word and a sentence one of your children might write.
- Have children say the word and decide on the beginning letters.
- Write the beginning letters on an index card.
- Take the index card with the beginning letters to the pocket chart and have children say the columns of rhymes and the new word to find the rhyming pattern.
- Write the rhyming pattern on the card to finish the word.
- Have students write the word on paper or a whiteboard.

# Lesson 57

## cheats

**Letters:** a  e  c  h  s  t  (Rhyming patterns **eat**, **at**, **each**)

**Make:** at  ate  eat  sat  hat  heat  seat  east  each  teach
cheat  cheats

**Sort:**

| eat | at | each |
|------|------|------|
| heat | hat | teach |
| seat | sat | |
| cheat | | |

**Transfer:** beat  beach  peach

## Make Words

- Have children name and hold up letters.
- Tell children how many letters to use to make each word.
- Have children say each word and stretch out some words.
- Give sentences to clarify meaning.
- Give specific instructions on how to change words:
  — Add one letter.
  — Change the first letter.
  — Use the same letters.
- Have children clear their holders before making an unrelated word.
- Have children correct their word once it is made in the pocket chart.
- Give children one minute to figure out the secret word and then give them clues.

## Sort Words

- Put words in pocket chart in the order made.
- Have children say and spell each word.
- Remind them of how each word was changed to spell the new word.
- Select one word from each rhyming set and line up in columns.
- Let children choose the other words that rhyme.
- Have children pronounce the words.

## Transfer Words

- Tell children that they are going to use the rhyming words to spell some new words they might need when they are writing.
- Say the word and a sentence one of your children might write.
- Have children say the word and decide on the beginning letters.
- Write the beginning letters on an index card.
- Take the index card with the beginning letters to the pocket chart and have children say the columns of rhymes and the new word to find the rhyming pattern.
- Write the rhyming pattern on the card to finish the word.
- Have students write the word on paper or a whiteboard.

# Lesson 58

## coats/coast/tacos

**Letters:** | a | o | c | s | t |  (Rhyming patterns **at**, **oat**)

This lesson has three secret words: **coats**, **coast**, and **tacos**.

**Make:**  at  sat  cat  cot  coat  oats  scat  cast  cost  coast  coats  tacos

**Sort:**
| | |
|---|---|
| at | oats |
| sat | coats |
| cat | |

**Transfer:**  boats    fat    flat

## Make Words

- Have children name and hold up letters.
- Tell children how many letters to use to make each word.
- Have children say each word and stretch out some words.
- Give sentences to clarify meaning.
- Give specific instructions on how to change words:
  — Add one letter.
  — Change the first letter.
  — Use the same letters.
- Have children clear their holders before making an unrelated word.
- Have children correct their word once it is made in the pocket chart.
- Tell children these letters make three secret words. Give children one minute to figure out the secret words and then give them clues.

## Sort Words

- Put words in pocket chart in the order made.
- Have children say and spell each word.
- Remind them of how each word was changed to spell the new word.
- Select one word from each rhyming set and line up in columns.
- Let children choose the other words that rhyme.
- Have children pronounce the words.

## Transfer Words

- Tell children that they are going to use the rhyming words spell to some new words they might need when they are writing.
- Say the word and a sentence one of your children might write.
- Have children say the word and decide on the beginning letters.
- Write the beginning letters on an index card.
- Take the index card with the beginning letters to the pocket chart and have children say the columns of rhymes and the new word to find the rhyming pattern.
- Write the rhyming pattern on the card to finish the word.
- Have students write the word on paper or a whiteboard.

# Lesson 59

## carrots

**Letters:** | a | o | c | r | r | s | t | (Rhyming patterns **oast**, **at**, **oat**, **ot**)

**Make:** cat  rat  rot  cot  cost  cast  coat  oats  coats  coast
roast  carrots

**Sort:**

| coast | cat | oats | rot |
|-------|-----|-------|-----|
| roast | rat | coats | cot |

**Transfer:** toast  trot  boats

## Make Words

- Have children name and hold up letters.
- Tell children how many letters to use to make each word.
- Have children say each word and stretch out some words.
- Give sentences to clarify meaning.
- Give specific instructions on how to change words:
  — Add one letter.
  — Change the first letter.
  — Use the same letters.
- Have children clear their holders before making an unrelated word.
- Have children correct their word once it is made in the pocket chart.
- Give children one minute to figure out the secret word and then give them clues.

## Sort Words

- Put words in pocket chart in the order made.
- Have children say and spell each word.
- Remind them of how each word was changed to spell the new word.
- Select one word from each rhyming set and line up in columns.
- Let children choose the other words that rhyme.
- Have children pronounce the words.

## Transfer Words

- Tell children that they are going to use the rhyming words to spell some new words they might need when they are writing.
- Say the word and a sentence one of your children might write.
- Have children say the word and decide on the beginning letters.
- Write the beginning letters on an index card.
- Take the index card with the beginning letters to the pocket chart and have children say the columns of rhymes and the new word to find the rhyming pattern.
- Write the rhyming pattern on the card to finish the word.
- Have students write the word on paper or a whiteboard.

## combat

**Letters:** a o b c m t (Rhyming patterns **at**, **oat**)

**Make:** am  at  bat  cat  cot  Tom  oat  boat  coat  moat  combat

**Sort:**

| at | oat |
|----|-----|
| bat | boat |
| cat | coat |
|    | moat |

**Transfer:** brat  float  throat

## Make Words

- Have children name and hold up letters.
- Tell children how many letters to use to make each word.
- Have children say each word and stretch out some words.
- Give sentences to clarify meaning.
- Give specific instructions on how to change words:
  — Add one letter.
  — Change the first letter.
  — Use the same letters.
- Have children clear their holders before making an unrelated word.
- Make sure children use a capital **T** when spelling the name **Tom**.
- Have children correct their word once it is made in the pocket chart.
- Give children one minute to figure out the secret word and then give them clues.

## Sort Words

- Put words in pocket chart in the order made.
- Have children say and spell each word.
- Remind them of how each word was changed to spell the new word.
- Select one word from each rhyming set and line up in columns.
- Let children choose the other words that rhyme.
- Have children pronounce the words.

## Transfer Words

- Tell children that they are going to use the rhyming words to spell some new words they might need when they are writing.
- Say the word and a sentence one of your children might write.
- Have children say the word and decide on the beginning letters.
- Write the beginning letters on an index card.
- Take the index card with the beginning letters to the pocket chart and have children say the columns of rhymes and the new word to find the rhyming pattern.
- Write the rhyming pattern on the card to finish the word.
- Have students write the word on paper or a whiteboard.

Tell the children to pretend they are writing a story and need to spell some words. To spell a word, they should stretch out the word and write the beginning letters and then decide which rhyming words will help them finish the word. Remind them that this is exactly what they do in the transfer step of each Making Words lesson but now you want to see if they can do it on their own.

Write these words in columns and have your children chorally pronounce and spell them. Have them notice that each column of words has the same letters from the vowel to the end of the words and that the words in the column rhyme.

| eat | but | am |
|------|------|-----|
| seat | cut | ham |
| meat | shut | Sam |

Have the children number a sheet of paper from 1 to 5. Say a word and put it in a sentence. Ask your students to stretch out each word to hear the beginning letters and then decide which words it rhymes with to finish spelling the word:

| nut | jam | slam | cheat | treat |
|------|------|------|--------|--------|

Record their responses on your record sheet. If students did not use the correct pattern or beginning letters, record what they did use and analyze their errors.

Child's Name _____

| Word | Beginning Letters | Rhyming Pattern |
|------|-------------------|-----------------|
| mop | m | op |
| tin | t | in |
| flat | fl | at |
| chin | ch | in |
| shop | sh | op |
| **After Lesson 60** | | |
| nut | n | ut |
| jam | j | am |
| slam | sl | am |
| cheat | ch | eat |
| treat | tr | eat |
| | | |
| | | |
| | | |
| | | |

# Lessons 61-70

These 10 lessons introduce the vowel pairs **ay**, **ai**, and **ue** and the vowel **y**. Children should notice that the **y** is a different color. Explain that sometimes **y** is a consonant and sometimes **y** is a vowel.

# Lesson 61
## stray/trays

**Letters:**   **a, r, s, t, y**   (The vowel pair **ay** is introduced.)

This lesson has two secret words: **stray** and **trays**.

**Words to Make:**   at   sat   say   Ray   rat   art   tar   star   stay
tray   stray   trays

## Part One • Making Words

Have the children arrange their letters in front of their holders to match the pocket-chart letters, with the vowel first and the other letters in alphabetical order.

Ask the children to hold up and name each letter and then begin making words.

**at**   "The first word we are going to spell is **at**. We are **at** school . Everyone say **at**. Use 2 letters to spell **at**."

Choose a child who has **at** spelled correctly to spell **at** with the pocket-chart letters. Have the class chorally spell **at** and fix their word if **at** is not correct.

**sat**   "Add 1 letter to spell **sat**. I **sat** in the front row. Everyone say **sat**."

Let a child who has **sat** spelled correctly spell **sat** with the pocket-chart letters.

**say**   "Change the last letter to spell **say**. We **say** the words we are spelling. Everyone say **say**."

Continue the lesson, giving children explicit instruction about which letters to re-move and where to add letters. Put each word in a sentence and have children say each word before making it. Have them "stretch" some words to provide practice for children who are still learning to segment words. Let a child who has spelled the word correctly come to the front of the room and make that word with the pocket-chart letters. Choose your struggling readers when the word is an easy word and choose your advanced readers for harder words. Have the children chorally spell each word after it is made in the pocket chart and fix their word to match.

| | |
|---|---|
| **Ray** | "Change the first letter to spell the name **Ray**. Do you know anyone named **Ray**? Everyone say **Ray**, and when you spell **Ray** remember **Ray** is a name." |
| **rat** | "Change the last letter to spell **rat**. Have you ever seen a **rat**? Everyone say **rat**." |
| **art** | "Use the same 3 letters to spell **art**. We all love **art**. Everyone say **art**." |
| **tar** | Use the same letters again to spell **tar**. Some roads are made of **tar**. Everyone say **tar**." |
| **star** | "Add a letter to spell **star**. I saw a very bright **star**. Everyone say **star**." |
| **stay** | "Change the last letter to spell **stay**. I told my dog to **stay**. Everyone say **stay**." |
| **tray** | "Change just the first 2 letters to spell **tray**. Put your food on your **tray**. Everyone say **tray**." |
| **stray** **trays** | **(two secret words)** "Today's letters spell two secret words. Move your letters in your holder and see if you can figure out the secret words. Signal me if you think you have one of them." |

If no one makes the secret words in one minute, give them clues.

End the making words part of the lesson by having both **trays** and **stray** spelled in the pocket chart and letting everyone hold up their holders to show you **trays** or **stray** made in their holders. Have them close the holders and turn their attention to the pocket chart.

# Part Two • Sorting Words (Sort for **at, ar, ay**)

Tell your students that they are going to say all the words they spelled and then sort the rhyming words. Using the index cards with the words, place them in the pocket chart and have the children pronounce them. Remind the children of what they changed to make each word.

"First we used 2 letters to spell **at**, **a-t**."

"We added an **s** to spell **sat**, **s-a-t**."

"We changed the last letter to a **y** to spell **say**, **s-a-y**."

"We changed the **s** to a capital R to spell the name **Ray**, **R-a-y**."

"We changed the last letter to spell **rat**, **r-a-t**."

"We used the same letters to spell **art**, **a-r-t**."

"We used the same letters again to spell **tar**, **t-a-r**."

"We added the **s** to spell **star**, **s-t-a-r**."

"We changed the last letter to spell **stay, s-t-a-y**."

"We changed the first 2 letters to spell **tray, t-r-a-y**."

"Today, we had two secret words: **stray, s-t-r-a-y** and **trays, t-r-a-y-s**."

"Now we need to sort out the rhymes. I will take one of each set and you can come and help me find the others."

Arrange one of each set of rhyming words to begin three columns.

**sat**        **tar**        **Ray**

Choose three children and help them choose the rhyming words and line them up in columns. Have the rhyming words pronounced and have children notice that they all rhyme and they all have the same letters from the vowel to the end of the word.

| **sat** | **tar** | **Ray** |
|---|---|---|
| **at** | **star** | **say** |
| **rat** | | **tray** |
| | | **stay** |
| | | **stray** |

# Part Three • Transfer   clay   Jay   spray

Have the children take out paper. Tell them that you are going to say a word that someone might be writing. By figuring out the rhyming pattern, they will be able to spell the word.

"The first word we are going to spell is **clay**. David might be writing about making something out of **clay**. Let's all say **clay** and listen for the beginning letters."

Write **cl** on an index card when the children decide that **clay** begins with **cl**. Take the index card to the pocket chart and have the children pronounce **clay** with each set of rhyming words. When they decide that **clay** rhymes with **Ray**, **say**, **tray**, **stay**, and **stray**, write **ay** next to **cl**. Have the children write **clay** on their papers.

Repeat this procedure for the name **Jay** and **spray**.

# Lesson 62
## Thursday

**Letters:** a u d h r s t y (Rhyming patterns **at**, **ad**, **ard**, **ay**)

**Make:** day hay hat sat sad had hard yard Ray tray stray Thursday

**Sort:**

| hat | sad | hard | day |
|-----|-----|------|-------|
| sat | had | yard | hay |
|     |     |      | tray |
|     |     |      | stray |

**Transfer:** card      glad      spray

## Make Words

- Have children name and hold up letters.
- Tell children how many letters to use to make each word.
- Have children say each word and stretch out some words.
- Give sentences to clarify meaning.
- Give specific instructions on how to change words:
  — Add one letter.
  — Change the first letter.
  — Use the same letters.
- Have children clear their holders before making an unrelated word.
- Be sure children use capital letters when spelling **Ray** and **Thursday**.
- Have children correct their word once it is made in the pocket chart.
- Give children one minute to figure out the secret word and then give them clues.

## Sort Words

- Put words in pocket chart in the order made.
- Have children say and spell each word.
- Remind them of how each word was changed to spell the new word.
- Select one word from each rhyming set and line up in columns.
- Let children choose the other words that rhyme.
- Have children pronounce the words.

## Transfer Words

- Tell children that they are going to use the rhyming words to spell some new words they might need when they are writing.
- Say the word and a sentence one of your children might write.
- Have children say the word and decide on the beginning letters.
- Write the beginning letters on an index card.
- Take the index card with the beginning letters to the pocket chart and have children say the columns of rhymes and the new word to find the rhyming pattern.
- Write the rhyming pattern on the card to finish the word.
- Have students write the word on paper or a whiteboard.

## paints

**Letters:** | a | i | n | p | s | t |   (The vowel pair **ai** is introduced.)

**Make:** in  an  ant  pan  pain  pant  Stan  stain  Spain  pants  paints

**Sort:**

| an | ant | stain |
|------|------|-------|
| pan | pant | Spain |
| Stan |  | pain |

**Transfer:** plant  chant  train

# Make Words

- Have children name and hold up letters.
- Tell children how many letters to use to make each word.
- Have children say each word and stretch out some words.
- Give sentences to clarify meaning.
- Give specific instructions on how to change words:
  — Add one letter.
  — Change the first letter.
  — Use the same letters.
- Have children clear their holders before making an unrelated word.
- Be sure children use capital letters when spelling **Stan** and **Spain**.
- Have children correct their word once it is made in the pocket chart.
- Give children one minute to figure out the secret word and then give them clues.

# Sort Words

- Put words in pocket chart in the order made.
- Have children say and spell each word.
- Remind them of how each word was changed to spell the new word.
- Select one word from each rhyming set and line up in columns.
- Let children choose the other words that rhyme.
- Have children pronounce the words.

# Transfer Words

- Tell children that they are going to use the rhyming words to spell some new words they might need when they are writing.
- Say the word and a sentence one of your children might write.
- Have children say the word and decide on the beginning letters.
- Write the beginning letters on an index card.
- Take the index card with the beginning letters to the pocket chart and have children say the columns of rhymes and the new word to find the rhyming pattern.
- Write the rhyming pattern on the card to finish the word.
- Have students write the word on paper or a whiteboard.

# Lesson 64
## animals

**Letters:** a a i l m n s (Rhyming patterns **an**, **am**, **ail**)

**Make:** Al an am Sam man main mail nail sail snail animal animals

**Sort:**

| an | Sam | mail |
|----|-----|------|
| man | am | nail |
| | | sail |
| | | snail |

**Transfer:** jail trail clam

## Make Words

- Have children name and hold up letters.
- Tell children how many letters to use to make each word.
- Have children say each word and stretch out some words.
- Give sentences to clarify meaning.
- Give specific instructions on how to change words:
  — Add one letter.
  — Change the first letter.
  — Use the same letters.
- Have children clear their holders before making an unrelated word.
- Be sure children use capital letters when spelling **Al** and **Sam**.
- Have children correct their word once it is made in the pocket chart.
- Give children one minute to figure out the secret word and then give them clues.

## Sort Words

- Put words in pocket chart in the order made.
- Have children say and spell each word.
- Remind them of how each word was changed to spell the new word.
- Select one word from each rhyming set and line up in columns.
- Let children choose the other words that rhyme.
- Have children pronounce the words.

## Transfer Words

- Tell children that they are going to use the rhyming words to spell some new words they might need when they are writing.
- Say the word and a sentence one of your children might write.
- Have children say the word and decide on the beginning letters.
- Write the beginning letters on an index card.
- Take the index card with the beginning letters to the pocket chart and have children say the columns of rhymes and the new word to find the rhyming pattern.
- Write the rhyming pattern on the card to finish the word.
- Have students write the word on paper or a whiteboard.

# Lesson 65

## jumpers

**Letters:** | e | u | j | m | p | r | s |   (The vowel team **u-e** is introduced.)

**Make:**   up   us   use   Sue   ump   jump   user   sure   pure   super
jumper   jumpers

**Sort:**   ump          sure
jump          pure

**Transfer:**   dump          cure          thump

## Make Words

- Have children name and hold up letters.
- Tell children how many letters to use to make each word.
- Have children say each word and stretch out some words.
- Give sentences to clarify meaning.
- Give specific instructions on how to change words:
  — Add one letter.
  — Change the first letter.
  — Use the same letters.
- Have children clear their holders before making an unrelated word.
- Be sure children use a capital letter when spelling **Sue**.
- Have children correct their word once it is made in the pocket chart.
- Give children one minute to figure out the secret word and then give them clues.

## Sort Words

- Put words in pocket chart in the order made.
- Have children say and spell each word.
- Remind them of how each word was changed to spell the new word.
- Select one word from each rhyming set and line up in columns.
- Let children choose the other words that rhyme.
- Have children pronounce the words.

## Transfer Words

- Tell children that they are going to use the rhyming words to spell some new words they might need when they are writing.
- Say the word and a sentence one of your children might write.
- Have children say the word and decide on the beginning letters.
- Write the beginning letters on an index card.
- Take the index card with the beginning letters to the pocket chart and have children say the columns of rhymes and the new word to find the rhyming pattern.
- Write the rhyming pattern on the card to finish the word.
- Have students write the word on paper or a whiteboard.

# Lesson 66

## students

**Letters:** `e` `u` `d` `n` `s` `s` `t` `t`   (Rhyming patterns **ue**, **un**)

**Make:**   us   use   Sue   due   sun   stun   nuts   dust   tunes   dunes
sunset   students

**Sort:**
| Sue | sun | tunes |
|-----|-----|-------|
| due | stun | dunes |

**Transfer:**   true   blue   prunes

## Make Words

- Have children name and hold up letters.
- Tell children how many letters to use to make each word.
- Have children say each word and stretch out some words.
- Give sentences to clarify meaning.
- Give specific instructions on how to change words:
  — Add one letter.
  — Change the first letter.
  — Use the same letters.
- Have children clear their holders before making an unrelated word.
- Be sure children use a capital letter when spelling **Sue**.
- Have children correct their word once it is made in the pocket chart.
- Give children one minute to figure out the secret word and then give them clues.

## Sort Words

- Put words in pocket chart in the order made.
- Have children say and spell each word.
- Remind them of how each word was changed to spell the new word.
- Select one word from each rhyming set and line up in columns.
- Let children choose the other words that rhyme.
- Have children pronounce the words.

## Transfer Words

- Tell children that they are going to use the rhyming words to spell some new words they might need when they are writing.
- Say the word and a sentence one of your children might write.
- Have children say the word and decide on the beginning letters.
- Write the beginning letters on an index card.
- Take the index card with the beginning letters to the pocket chart and have children say the columns of rhymes and the new word to find the rhyming pattern.
- Write the rhyming pattern on the card to finish the word.
- Have students write the word on paper or a whiteboard.

# Lesson 67

## pictures

**Letters:** e  i  u  c  p  r  s  t   (Rhyming patterns **ure**, **up**, **ue**)

**Make:**  up  us  use  Sue  cup  sure  pure  cure  cute  true  super  pictures

**Sort:**

| sure | up | true |
|------|-----|------|
| cure | cup | Sue |
| pure | | |

**Transfer:**  blue      clue      pup

## Make Words

- Have children name and hold up letters.
- Tell children how many letters to use to make each word.
- Have children say each word and stretch out some words.
- Give sentences to clarify meaning.
- Give specific instructions on how to change words:
  — Add one letter.
  — Change the first letter.
  — Use the same letters.
- Have children clear their holders before making an unrelated word.
- Be sure children use a capital letter when spelling **Sue**.
- Have children correct their word once it is made in the pocket chart.
- Give children one minute to figure out the secret word and then give them clues.

## Sort Words

- Put words in pocket chart in the order made.
- Have children say and spell each word.
- Remind them of how each word was changed to spell the new word.
- Select one word from each rhyming set and line up in columns.
- Let children choose the other words that rhyme.
- Have children pronounce the words.

## Transfer Words

- Tell children that they are going to use the rhyming words to spell some new words they might need when they are writing.
- Say the word and a sentence one of your children might write.
- Have children say the word and decide on the beginning letters.
- Write the beginning letters on an index card.
- Take the index card with the beginning letters to the pocket chart and have children say the columns of rhymes and the new word to find the rhyming pattern.
- Write the rhyming pattern on the card to finish the word.
- Have students write the word on paper or a whiteboard.

# Lesson 68

## Friday

**Letters:** a i d f r y (Rhyming patterns **ay**, **y**)

**Make:** if   day   Ray   Fay   far   dry   fry   air   fair   fairy   dairy   Friday

**Sort:**
| day | dry | fair | fairy |
|-----|-----|------|-------|
| Ray | fry | air | dairy |
| Fay | | | |

**Transfer:** cry   spray   shy

## Make Words

- Have children name and hold up letters.
- Tell children how many letters to use to make each word.
- Have children say each word and stretch out some words.
- Give sentences to clarify meaning.
- Give specific instructions on how to change words:
  — Add one letter.
  — Change the first letter.
  — Use the same letters.
- Have children clear their holders before making an unrelated word.
- Be sure children use capital letters when spelling **Ray**, **Fay**, and **Friday**.
- Have children correct their word once it is made in the pocket chart.
- Tell children these letters make three secret words. Give children one minute to figure out the secret words and then give them clues.

## Sort Words

- Put words in pocket chart in the order made.
- Have children say and spell each word.
- Remind them of how each word was changed to spell the new word.
- Select one word from each rhyming set and line up in columns.
- Let children choose the other words that rhyme.
- Have children pronounce the words.

## Transfer Words

- Tell children that they are going to use the rhyming words to spell some new words they might need when they are writing.
- Say the word and a sentence one of your children might write.
- Have children say the word and decide on the beginning letters.
- Write the beginning letters on an index card.
- Take the index card with the beginning letters to the pocket chart and have children say the columns of rhymes and the new word to find the rhyming pattern.
- Write the rhyming pattern on the card to finish the word.
- Have students write the word on paper or a whiteboard.

# Lesson 69
## Saturday

**Letters:** a a u d r s t y  (Rhyming patterns **ust**, **ay**, **y**)

**Make:** say  day  dry  try  tray  dust  rust  rusty  dusty  study  sturdy  Saturday

**Sort:**

| dust | say | try | dusty |
|------|-----|-----|-------|
| rust | day | dry | rusty |
|      | tray |    |       |

**Transfer:** must    just    trust

## Make Words

- Have children name and hold up letters.
- Tell children how many letters to use to make each word.
- Have children say each word and stretch out some words.
- Give sentences to clarify meaning.
- Give specific instructions on how to change words:
  — Add one letter.
  — Change the first letter.
  — Use the same letters.
- Have children clear their holders before making an unrelated word.
- Be sure children use a capital letter when spelling **Saturday**.
- Have children correct their word once it is made in the pocket chart.
- Give children one minute to figure out the secret word and then give them clues.

## Sort Words

- Put words in pocket chart in the order made.
- Have children say and spell each word.
- Remind them of how each word was changed to spell the new word.
- Select one word from each rhyming set and line up in columns.
- Let children choose the other words that rhyme.
- Have children pronounce the words.

## Transfer Words

- Tell children that they are going to use the rhyming words to spell some new words they might need when they are writing.
- Say the word and a sentence one of your children might write.
- Have children say the word and decide on the beginning letters.
- Write the beginning letters on an index card.
- Take the index card with the beginning letters to the pocket chart and have children say the columns of rhymes and the new word to find the rhyming pattern.
- Write the rhyming pattern on the card to finish the word.
- Have students write the word on paper or a whiteboard.

# Lesson 70

## backyard

**Letters:** a a b c d k r y  (Rhyming patterns **ay, ack, ark, y**)

**Make:**  by  cry  dry  day  Ray  Kay  dark  bark  back  rack  yard  backyard

**Sort:**

| | | | |
|---|---|---|---|
| by | Ray | rack | dark |
| cry | day | back | bark |
| dry | Kay | | |

**Transfer:**  park  black  shark

## Make Words

- Have children name and hold up letters.
- Tell children how many letters to use to make each word.
- Have children say each word and stretch out some words.
- Give sentences to clarify meaning.
- Give specific instructions on how to change words:
  — Add one letter.
  — Change the first letter.
  — Use the same letters.
- Have children clear their holders before making an unrelated word.
- Be sure children spell names with capital letters.
- Have children correct their word once it is made in the pocket chart.
- Give children one minute to figure out the secret word and then give them clues.

## Sort Words

- Put words in pocket chart in the order made.
- Have children say and spell each word.
- Remind them of how each word was changed to spell the new word.
- Select one word from each rhyming set and line up in columns.
- Let children choose the other words that rhyme.
- Have children pronounce the words.

## Transfer Words

- Tell children that they are going to use the rhyming words to spell some new words they might need when they are writing.
- Say the word and a sentence one of your children might write.
- Have children say the word and decide on the beginning letters.
- Write the beginning letters on an index card.
- Take the index card with the beginning letters to the pocket chart and have children say the columns of rhymes and the new word to find the rhyming pattern.
- Write the rhyming pattern on the card to finish the word.
- Have students write the word on paper or a whiteboard.

Tell the children to pretend they are writing a story and need to spell some words. To spell a word, they should stretch out the word and write the beginning letters and then decide which rhyming words will help them finish the word. Remind them that this is exactly what they do in the transfer step of each Making Words lesson but now you want to see if they can do it on their own.

Write these words in columns and have your children chorally pronounce and spell them. Have them notice that each column of words has the same letters from the vowel to the end of the words and that the words in the column rhyme.

| may | my | rain |
|-----|-----|------|
| pay | cry | main |
| play | try | train |

Have the children number a sheet of paper from 1 to 5. Say a word and put it in a sentence. Ask your students to stretch out each word to hear the beginning letters and then decide which words it rhymes with to finish spelling the word:

**stay**      **dry**      **brain**      **gray**      **chain**

Record their responses on your record sheet. If students did not use the correct pattern or beginning letters, record what they did use and analyze their errors.

Child's Name _____

| Word | Beginning Letters | Rhyming Pattern |
|------|-------------------|-----------------|
| **After Lesson 50** | | |
| mop | m | op |
| tin | t | in |
| flat | fl | at |
| chin | ch | in |
| shop | sh | op |
| **After Lesson 60** | | |
| nut | n | ut |
| jam | j | am |
| slam | sl | am |
| cheat | ch | eat |
| treat | tr | eat |
| **After Lesson 70** | | |
| stay | st | ay |
| dry | dr | y |
| brain | br | ain |
| gray | gr | ay |
| chain | ch | ain |

# Lessons 71-80

In these lessons, students learn to decode and spell words with **i-e**, **igh**, and **a-e**. The consonant **z** is also taught.

## Lesson 71

## things

**Letters:**   **i, g, h, n, s, t**   (Rhyming pattern **ight** is introduced.)

**Words to Make:**   **sit   hit   tin   thin   hint   sing   sting   thing   night sight   things**

## Part One • Making Words

 Have the children arrange their letters in front of their holders to match the pocket-chart letters, with the vowel first and the other letters in alphabetical order.

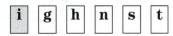

Ask the children to hold up and name each letter and then begin making words.

**sit**       "The first word we are going to spell is **sit**. Who do you like to **sit** next to? Everyone say **sit**. Use 3 letters to spell **sit**."

Choose a child who has **sit** spelled correctly to spell **sit** with the pocket-chart letters. Have the class chorally spell **sit** and fix their word if **sit** is not correct.

**hit**       "Change 1 letter to spell **hit**. The batter **hit** the ball. Everyone say **hit**."

Let a child who has **hit** spelled correctly spell **hit** with the pocket-chart letters.

**tin**       "Start over and use three letters to spell **tin**. We recycle **tin** cans. Everyone say **tin**."

Continue the lesson, giving children explicit instruction about which letters to remove and where to add letters. Put each word in a sentence and have children say each word before making it. Have them "stretch" some words to provide practice for children who are still learning to segment words. Let a child who has spelled the word correctly come to the front of the room and make that word with the pocket-chart letters. Choose

your struggling readers when the word is an easy word and choose your advanced readers for harder words. Have the children chorally spell each word after it is made in the pocket chart and fix their word to match.

| | |
|---|---|
| **thin** | "Add a letter to tin to spell **thin**. I like **thin** crust pizza. Everyone say **thin**." |
| **hint** | "Move the letters to spell **hint**. Can you give me a **hint** about my birthday present? Everyone say **hint**." |
| **this** | "Clear your holders and use 4 letters to spell **this**. **This** is our classroom. Everyone say **this**." |
| **sing** | Clear your holders again and use 4 letters to spell **sing**. I **sing** in the shower. Everyone say **sing**." |
| **sting** | "Add a letter to spell **sting**. A bee can **sting** you. Everyone say **sting**." |
| **thing** | "Change the first 2 letters to spell **thing**. What is that funny-looking **thing**? Everyone say **thing**." |
| **night** | "Use the same letters to spell **night**. It gets dark at **night**. Everyone say **night**." |
| **sight** | "Change just the first letter to spell **sight**. My grandpa is almost blind and is losing his **sight**. Everyone say **sight**." |
| **things** | **(secret word)** "Move your letters in your holder and see if you can figure out the secret word. Signal me if you think you have figured it out." |

If no one makes the secret word in one minute, give them clues.

End the making words part of the lesson by having **things** spelled in the pocket chart and letting everyone hold up their holders to show you **things** made in their holders. Have them close the holders and turn their attention to the pocket chart.

## Part Two • Sorting Words (Sort for **in**, **ing**, **it**, **ight**)

Tell your students that they are going to say all the words they spelled and then sort the rhyming words. Using the index cards with the words, place them in the pocket chart and have the children pronounce them. Remind the children of what they changed to make each word.

"First we used 3 letters to spell **sit**, **s-i-t**."

"We changed the first letter to spell **hit**, **h-i-t**."

"We spelled another 3 letter word, **tin**, **t-i-n**."

"We added a letter to spell **thin**, **t-h-i-n**."

"We used the same letters to spell **hint**, **h-i-n-t**."

"We used 4 letters to spell **this**, **t-h-i-s**."

"We used 4 letters to spell **sing**, **s-i-n-g**."

"We added the **t** to spell **sting**, **s-t-i-n-g**."

"We changed the first 2 letters to spell **thing**, **t-h-i-n-g**."

"We moved the letters to spell **night**, **n-i-g-h-t**.

"We changed the first letter to spell **sight**, **s-i-g-h-t**."

"We used all our letters to spell the secret word, **things**, **t-h-i-n-g-s**."

"Now we need to sort out the rhymes. I will take one of each set and you can come and help me find the others."

Arrange one of each set of rhyming words to begin three columns.

**tin**      **sing**      **sit**      **night**

Choose three children and help them choose the rhyming words and line them up in columns. Have the rhyming words pronounced and have children notice that they all rhyme and they all have the same letters from the vowel to the end of the word.

| **tin** | **sing** | **sit** | **night** |
|---|---|---|---|
| **thin** | **sting** | **hit** | **sight** |
| **thing** | | | |

# Part Three ● Transfer   king  spin  bright

Have the children take out paper. Tell them that you are going to say a word that someone might be writing. By figuring out the rhyming pattern, they will be able to spell the word.

"The first word we are going to spell is **king**. Kathleen might be writing a story about a **king**. Let's all say **king** and listen for the beginning letters."

Write **k** on an index card when the children decide that **king** begins with **k**. Take the index card to the pocket chart and have the children pronounce **king** with each set of rhyming words. When they decide that **king** rhymes with **sing**, **sting**, and **thing**, write **ing** next to **k**. Have children write **king** on their papers.

Repeat this procedure for **spin** and **bright**.

# Lesson 72

## winners

**Letters:** `e` `i` `n` `n` `r` `s` `w`  (The vowel team **i-e** is introduced.)

**Make:**  is   in   win   sir   wire   rise   wise   wiser   siren   winners

**Sort:**
| | |
|---|---|
| in | rise |
| win | wise |

**Transfer:**  grin        spin        twin

## Make Words

- Have children name and hold up letters.
- Tell children how many letters to use to make each word.
- Have children say each word and stretch out some words.
- Give sentences to clarify meaning.
- Give specific instructions on how to change words:
  — Add one letter.
  — Change the first letter.
  — Use the same letters.
- Have children clear their holders before making an unrelated word.
- Have children correct their word once it is made in the pocket chart.
- Give children one minute to figure out the secret word and then give them clues.

## Sort Words

- Put words in pocket chart in the order made.
- Have children say and spell each word.
- Remind them of how each word was changed to spell the new word.
- Select one word from each rhyming set and line up in columns.
- Let children choose the other words that rhyme.
- Have children pronounce the words.

## Transfer Words

- Tell children that they are going to use the rhyming words to spell some new words they might need when they are writing.
- Say the word and a sentence one of your children might write.
- Have children say the word and decide on the beginning letters.
- Write the beginning letters on an index card.
- Take the index card with the beginning letters to the pocket chart and have children say the columns of rhymes and the new word to find the rhyming pattern.
- Write the rhyming pattern on the card to finish the word.
- Have students write the word on paper or a whiteboard.

# Lesson 73

## zippered

**Letters:** e e i d p p z r  (The consonant **z** is introduced; rhyming patterns **ip**, **ipe**, **ide** )

**Make:** dip   zip   rip   drip   pipe   ripe   ride   pride   prize   dipper
zipper   zippered

**Sort:**

| dip | pipe | pride | zipper |
|-----|------|-------|--------|
| rip | ripe | ride | dipper |
| zip | | pride | |
| drip | | | |

**Transfer:** wipe   bride   glide

## Make Words

- Have children name and hold up letters.
- Tell children how many letters to use to make each word.
- Have children say each word and stretch out some words.
- Give sentences to clarify meaning.
- Give specific instructions on how to change words:
  — Add one letter.
  — Change the first letter.
  — Use the same letters.
- Have children clear their holders before making an unrelated word.
- Have children correct their word once it is made in the pocket chart.
- Give children one minute to figure out the secret word and then give them clues.

## Sort Words

- Put words in pocket chart in the order made.
- Have children say and spell each word.
- Remind them of how each word was changed to spell the new word.
- Select one word from each rhyming set and line up in columns.
- Let children choose the other words that rhyme.
- Have children pronounce the words.

## Transfer Words

- Tell children that they are going to use the rhyming words to spell some new words they might need when they are writing.
- Say the word and a sentence one of your children might write.
- Have children say the word and decide on the beginning letters.
- Write the beginning letters on an index card.
- Take the index card with the beginning letters to the pocket chart and have children say the columns of rhymes and the new word to find the rhyming pattern.
- Write the rhyming pattern on the card to finish the word.
- Have students write the word on paper or a whiteboard.

# Lesson 74

## fighters

**Letters:** | e | i | f | g | h | r | s | t | (Rhyming patterns **ir**, **ight**, **it**, **ire**)

**Make:** fit sit sir stir tire fire fist first shirt right fight fighters

**Sort:**

| sir | fight | sit | fire |
|------|-------|-----|------|
| stir | right | fit | tire |

**Transfer:** wire      lit      light

## Make Words

- Have children name and hold up letters.
- Tell children how many letters to use to make each word.
- Have children say each word and stretch out some words.
- Give sentences to clarify meaning.
- Give specific instructions on how to change words:
  — Add one letter.
  — Change the first letter.
  — Use the same letters.
- Have children clear their holders before making an unrelated word.
- Have children correct their word once it is made in the pocket chart.
- Give children one minute to figure out the secret word and then give them clues.

## Sort Words

- Put words in pocket chart in the order made.
- Have children say and spell each word.
- Remind them of how each word was changed to spell the new word.
- Select one word from each rhyming set and line up in columns.
- Let children choose the other words that rhyme.
- Have children pronounce the words.

## Transfer Words

- Tell children that they are going to use the rhyming words to spell some new words they might need when they are writing.
- Say the word and a sentence one of your children might write.
- Have children say the word and decide on the beginning letters.
- Write the beginning letters on an index card.
- Take the index card with the beginning letters to the pocket chart and have children say the columns of rhymes and the new word to find the rhyming pattern.
- Write the rhyming pattern on the card to finish the word.
- Have students write the word on paper or a whiteboard.

# Lesson 75
## plates

**Letters:** | a | e | l | p | s | t |   (The vowel team **a-e** is introduced.)

**Make:**  at  Pat  sat  ate  late  tale  pale  last  past  paste  plate  plates

**Sort:**

| at | late | pale | past |
|----|------|------|------|
| Pat | ate | tale | last |
| sat | plate | | |

**Transfer:**  state  scale  gate

## Make Words

- Have children name and hold up letters.
- Tell children how many letters to use to make each word.
- Have children say each word and stretch out some words.
- Give sentences to clarify meaning.
- Give specific instructions on how to change words:
  — Add one letter.
  — Change the first letter.
  — Use the same letters.
- Have children clear their holders before making an unrelated word.
- Be sure children use a capital letter when spelling the name **Pat**.
- Have children correct their word once it is made in the pocket chart.
- Give children one minute to figure out the secret word and then give them clues.

## Sort Words

- Put words in pocket chart in the order made.
- Have children say and spell each word.
- Remind them of how each word was changed to spell the new word.
- Select one word from each rhyming set and line up in columns.
- Let children choose the other words that rhyme.
- Have children pronounce the words.

## Transfer Words

- Tell children that they are going to use the rhyming words to spell some new words they might need when they are writing.
- Say the word and a sentence one of your children might write.
- Have children say the word and decide on the beginning letters.
- Write the beginning letters on an index card.
- Take the index card with the beginning letters to the pocket chart and have children say the columns of rhymes and the new word to find the rhyming pattern.
- Write the rhyming pattern on the card to finish the word.
- Have students write the word on paper or a whiteboard.

# Lesson 76
## strange

**Letters:** | a | e | g | n | r | s | t | (The two sounds of **g**)

**Make:** at ate age rag rat Nat Nate rate rage stage range strange

**Sort:**

| rat | age | ate | range |
|-----|------|------|---------|
| at | rage | Nate | strange |
| Nat | stage | rate | |

**Transfer:** cage    skate    page

## Make Words

- Have children name and hold up letters.
- Tell children how many letters to use to make each word.
- Have children say each word and stretch out some words.
- Give sentences to clarify meaning.
- Give specific instructions on how to change words:
  — Add one letter.
  — Change the first letter.
  — Use the same letters.
- Have children clear their holders before making an unrelated word.
- Be sure children use capital letters when spelling names.
- Have children correct their word once it is made in the pocket chart.
- Give children one minute to figure out the secret word and then give them clues.

## Sort Words

- Put words in pocket chart in the order made.
- Have children say and spell each word.
- Remind them of how each word was changed to spell the new word.
- Select one word from each rhyming set and line up in columns.
- Let children choose the other words that rhyme.
- Have children pronounce the words.

## Transfer Words

- Tell children that they are going to use the rhyming words to spell some new words they might need when they are writing.
- Say the word and a sentence one of your children might write.
- Have children say the word and decide on the beginning letters.
- Write the beginning letters on an index card.
- Take the index card with the beginning letters to the pocket chart and have children say the columns of rhymes and the new word to find the rhyming pattern.
- Write the rhyming pattern on the card to finish the word.
- Have students write the word on paper or a whiteboard.

# Lesson 77

## jacket

**Letters:** a e c j k t (Rhyming patterns **at**, **ate**, **ake**, **ack**)

**Make:** at act cat ate Kate take cake Jake tack Jack jacket

**Sort:**

| | | | |
|---|---|---|---|
| ate | at | cake | Jack |
| Kate | cat | take | tack |
| | | Jake | |

**Transfer:** cage    skate    page

## Make Words

- Have children name and hold up letters.
- Tell children how many letters to use to make each word.
- Have children say each word and stretch out some words.
- Give sentences to clarify meaning.
- Give specific instructions on how to change words:
  — Add one letter.
  — Change the first letter.
  — Use the same letters.
- Have children clear their holders before making an unrelated word.
- Be sure children use capital letters when spelling names.
- Have children correct their word once it is made in the pocket chart.
- Give children one minute to figure out the secret word and then give them clues.

## Sort Words

- Put words in pocket chart in the order made.
- Have children say and spell each word.
- Remind them of how each word was changed to spell the new word.
- Select one word from each rhyming set and line up in columns.
- Let children choose the other words that rhyme.
- Have children pronounce the words.

## Transfer Words

- Tell children that they are going to use the rhyming words to spell some new words they might need when they are writing.
- Say the word and a sentence one of your children might write.
- Have children say the word and decide on the beginning letters.
- Write the beginning letters on an index card.
- Take the index card with the beginning letters to the pocket chart and have children say the columns of rhymes and the new word to find the rhyming pattern.
- Write the rhyming pattern on the card to finish the word.
- Have students write the word on paper or a whiteboard.

## players

**Letters:**  a  e  l  p  r  s  y    (Rhyming patterns **at**, **ate**, **ay**, **ale**)

**Make:**    at   ate   say   Ray   rat   pal   pale   sale   rate   play   replay   players

**Sort:**

| ate | Ray | pale | at |
|-----|-----|------|-----|
| rate | play | sale | rat |
|  | say |  |  |

**Transfer:**   tray      stray      crate

## Make Words

- Have children name and hold up letters.
- Tell children how many letters to use to make each word.
- Have children say each word and stretch out some words.
- Give sentences to clarify meaning.
- Give specific instructions on how to change words:
  — Add one letter.
  — Change the first letter.
  — Use the same letters.
- Have children clear their holders before making an unrelated word.
- Be sure children use a capital letter when spelling the name **Ray**.
- Have children correct their word once it is made in the pocket chart.
- Tell children these letters make three secret words. Give children one minute to figure out the secret words and then give them clues.

## Sort Words

- Put words in pocket chart in the order made.
- Have children say and spell each word.
- Remind them of how each word was changed to spell the new word.
- Select one word from each rhyming set and line up in columns.
- Let children choose the other words that rhyme.
- Have children pronounce the words.

## Transfer Words

- Tell children that they are going to use the rhyming words to spell some new words they might need when they are writing.
- Say the word and a sentence one of your children might write.
- Have children say the word and decide on the beginning letters.
- Write the beginning letters on an index card.
- Take the index card with the beginning letters to the pocket chart and have children say the columns of rhymes and the new word to find the rhyming pattern.
- Write the rhyming pattern on the card to finish the word.
- Have students write the word on paper or a whiteboard.

# Lesson 79

## parents

**Letters:** | a | e | n | p | r | s | t | (Rhyming patterns **at**, **ate**, **ap**, **ape**)

**Make:** at   ate   ape   rat   rap   tap   tape   trap   rate   past   paste   **parents**

**Sort:**

| ate | rap | at | ape |
|------|------|------|------|
| rate | tap | rat | tape |
| | trap | | |

**Transfer:** grape     lap     shape

## Make Words

- Have children name and hold up letters.
- Tell children how many letters to use to make each word.
- Have children say each word and stretch out some words.
- Give sentences to clarify meaning.
- Give specific instructions on how to change words:
  — Add one letter.
  — Change the first letter.
  — Use the same letters.
- Have children clear their holders before making an unrelated word.
- Have children correct their word once it is made in the pocket chart.
- Give children one minute to figure out the secret word and then give them clues.

## Sort Words

- Put words in pocket chart in the order made.
- Have children say and spell each word.
- Remind them of how each word was changed to spell the new word.
- Select one word from each rhyming set and line up in columns.
- Let children choose the other words that rhyme.
- Have children pronounce the words.

## Transfer Words

- Tell children that they are going to use the rhyming words to spell some new words they might need when they are writing.
- Say the word and a sentence one of your children might write.
- Have children say the word and decide on the beginning letters.
- Write the beginning letters on an index card.
- Take the index card with the beginning letters to the pocket chart and have children say the columns of rhymes and the new word to find the rhyming pattern.
- Write the rhyming pattern on the card to finish the word.
- Have students write the word on paper or a whiteboard.

# Lesson 80
## pancakes

**Letters:** | a | a | e | c | k | n | p | s |  (Rhyming patterns **an**, **ack**, **ake**)

**Make:** an  pan  can  cap  cape  cane  cake  pack  sack  snack
snake  pancakes

**Sort:**

| an | pack | cake |
|------|-------|-------|
| pan | sack | snake |
| can | snack | |

**Transfer:** black  shack  crack

## Make Words

- Have children name and hold up letters.
- Tell children how many letters to use to make each word.
- Have children say each word and stretch out some words.
- Give sentences to clarify meaning.
- Give specific instructions on how to change words:
  — Add one letter.
  — Change the first letter.
  — Use the same letters.
- Have children clear their holders before making an unrelated word.
- Have children correct their word once it is made in the pocket chart.
- Give children one minute to figure out the secret word and then give them clues.

## Sort Words

- Put words in pocket chart in the order made.
- Have children say and spell each word.
- Remind them of how each word was changed to spell the new word.
- Select one word from each rhyming set and line up in columns.
- Let children choose the other words that rhyme.
- Have children pronounce the words.

## Transfer Words

- Tell children that they are going to use the rhyming words to spell some new words they might need when they are writing.
- Say the word and a sentence one of your children might write.
- Have children say the word and decide on the beginning letters.
- Write the beginning letters on an index card.
- Take the index card with the beginning letters to the pocket chart and have children say the columns of rhymes and the new word to find the rhyming pattern.
- Write the rhyming pattern on the card to finish the word.
- Have students write the word on paper or a whiteboard.

# Assessment Lessons 71-80

Write these words in columns and have your children chorally pronounce and spell them.

|  |  |  |
|---|---|---|
| back | make | right |
| black | take | night |
| pack | wake | might |

Have the children number a sheet of paper from 1 to 5. Say a word and put it in a sentence. Ask your students to stretch out each word to hear the beginning letters and then decide which words it rhymes with to finish spelling the word:

**track**     **bright**     **shake**     **snack**     **fight**

Record their responses on your record sheet. If students did not use the correct pattern or beginning letters, record what they did use and analyze their errors.

Child's Name _____

| Word | Beginning Letters | Rhyming Pattern |
|---|---|---|
| **After Lesson 50** | | |
| mop | m | op |
| tin | t | in |
| flat | fl | at |
| chin | ch | in |
| shop | sh | op |
| **After Lesson 60** | | |
| nut | n | ut |
| jam | j | am |
| slam | sl | am |
| cheat | ch | eat |
| treat | tr | eat |

| Word | Beginning Letters | Rhyming Pattern |
|---|---|---|
| **After Lesson 70** | | |
| stay | st | ay |
| dry | dr | y |
| brain | br | ain |
| gray | gr | ay |
| chain | ch | ain |
| **After Lesson 80** | | |
| track | tr | ack |
| bright | br | ight |
| snack | sn | ack |
| shake | sh | ake |
| fight | f | ight |

# Lessons 81-90

In these lessons, students learn to decode and spell words with **or** and **o-e** and words with the **all**, **ell**, and **ill** patterns.

## Lesson 81

### reports

**Letters:**  e, o, p, r, r, s, t   (The **or** combination is introduced.)

**Words to Make:**  top  pot  spot  stop  sort  port  sore  tore  store  sport  report  reports

## Part One • Making Words

 Have the children arrange their letters in front of their holders to match the pocket-chart letters, with the vowel first and the other letters in alphabetical order.

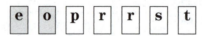

Ask the children to hold up and name each letter and then begin making words.

**top**    "The first word we are going to spell is **top**. Put your hand on **top** of your head. Everyone say **top**. Use 3 letters to spell **top**."

Choose a child who has **top** spelled correctly to spell **top** with the pocket-chart letters. Have the class chorally spell **top** and fix their word if **top** is not correct.

**pot**    "Move the letters to spell **pot**. I planted some flowers in a **pot**. Everyone say **pot**."

Let a child who has **pot** spelled correctly spell **pot** with the pocket-chart letters.

**spot**    "Add 1 letter to spell **spot**. Do you have a favorite **spot** on the carpet? Everyone say **spot**."

Continue the lesson, giving children explicit instruction about which letters to remove and where to add letters. Put each word in a sentence and have children say each word before making it. Have them "stretch" some words to provide practice for children who are still learning to segment words. Let a child who has spelled the word correctly come to the front of the room and make that word with the pocket-chart letters. Choose

your struggling readers when the word is an easy word and choose your advanced readers for harder words. Have the children chorally spell each word after it is made in the pocket chart and fix their word to match.

| | |
|---|---|
| **stop** | "Move the letters to spell **stop**. We **stop** at a **stop** sign. Everyone say **stop**." |
| **sort** | "Use 4 letters to spell **sort**. After we make words, we **sort** then into patterns. Everyone say **sort**." |
| **port** | "Change 1 letter to spell **port**. A big ship docked at the **port**. Everyone say **port**." |
| **sore** | "Clear your holders again and use 4 letters to spell **sore**. My legs were **sore** after I finished the race. Everyone say **sore**." |
| **tore** | "Change a letter to spell **tore**. The baby **tore** the pages in the books. Everyone say **tore**." |
| **store** | "Add 1 letter to spell **store**. What **store** do you shop in? Everyone say **store**." |
| **sport** | "Use 5 letters to spell **sport**. Basketball is my favorite **sport**. Everyone say **sport**." |
| **report** | "Use 6 letters to spell **report**. Did you get good grades on your **report** card? Everyone say **report**." |
| **reports** | **(secret word)** "I bet most of you can figure out the secret word today. Make it in your holder and signal me if you think you have figured it out." |

If no one makes the secret word in one minute, give them clues.

End the making words part of the lesson by having **reports** spelled in the pocket chart and letting everyone hold up their holders to show you **reports** made in their holders. Have them close the holders and turn their attention to the pocket chart.

# Part Two • Sorting Words (Sort for patterns **ort**, **ore**, **op**, **ot**)

Using the index cards with the words, place them in the pocket chart and have the children pronounce them. Remind the children of what they changed to make each word.

"First we used 3 letters to spell **top**, **t-o-p**."

"We changed the first letter to spell **pot**, **p-o-t**."

"We added the **s** to spell **spot**, **s-p-o-t**."

"We used the same letters to spell **stop**, **s-t-o-p**."

"We used 4 letters to spell **sort**, **s-o-r-t**."

"We changed the **s** to a **p** to spell **port**, **p-o-r-t**."

"We used 4 letters to spell **sore**, **s-o-r-e**."

"We changed the first letter to spell **tore**, **t-o-r-e**."

"We added the **t** to spell **store**, **s-t-o-r-e**."

"We used 5 letters to spell **sport**, **s-p-o-r-t**.

"We used 6 letters to spell **report**, **r-e-p-o-r-t**."

"We added the **s** to spell the secret word, **reports**, **r-e-p-o-r-t-s**."

"Now we need to sort out the rhymes. I will take one of each set and you can come and help me find the others."

Arrange one of each set of rhyming words to begin four columns.

**port**      **sore**      **top**      **pot**

Choose four children and help them choose the rhyming words and line them up in columns. Have the rhyming words pronounced and have children notice that they all rhyme and they all have the same letters from the vowel to the end of the word.

| | | | |
|---|---|---|---|
| **port** | **sore** | **top** | **pot** |
| **sort** | **tore** | **stop** | **spot** |
| **sport** | **store** | | |

# Part Three ● Transfer   shop   short   shore

Have the children take out paper. Tell them that you are going to say a word that someone might be writing. By figuring out the rhyming pattern, they will be able to spell the word.

"The first word we are going to spell is **short**. Ramona might be writing that she likes to **shop**. Let's all say **shop** and listen for the beginning letters."

Write **sh** on an index card when the children decide that **shop** begins with **sh**. Take the index card to the pocket chart and have the children pronounce **shop** with each set of rhyming words. When they decide that **shop** rhymes with top and stop, write **op** next to **sh**. Have children write **shop** on their papers.

Repeat this procedure for **short** and **shore**.

# Lesson 82

## spoken

**Letters:** | e | o | k | n | p | s |  (The vowel team **o-e** is introduced.)

**Make:** no  so  son  Ken  pen  open  nose  pose  poke  pokes
spoke  spoken

**Sort:**

| no | pen | nose | spoke |
|----|-----|------|-------|
| so | Ken | pose | poke |

**Transfer:** rose      joke      choke

## Make Words

- Have children name and hold up letters.
- Tell children how many letters to use to make each word.
- Have children say each word and stretch out some words.
- Give sentences to clarify meaning.
- Give specific instructions on how to change words:
  — Add one letter.
  — Change the first letter.
  — Use the same letters.
- Have children clear their holders before making an unrelated word.
- Be sure children use a capital **K** when spelling the name **Ken**.
- Have children correct their word once it is made in the pocket chart.
- Give children one minute to figure out the secret word and then give them clues.

## Sort Words

- Put words in pocket chart in the order made.
- Have children say and spell each word.
- Remind them of how each word was changed to spell the new word.
- Select one word from each rhyming set and line up in columns.
- Let children choose the other words that rhyme.
- Have children pronounce the words.

## Transfer Words

- Tell children that they are going to use the rhyming words spell to some new words they might need when they are writing.
- Say the word and a sentence one of your children might write.
- Have children say the word and decide on the beginning letters.
- Write the beginning letters on an index card.
- Take the index card with the beginning letters to the pocket chart and have children say the columns of rhymes and the new word to find the rhyming pattern.
- Write the rhyming pattern on the card to finish the word.
- Have students write the word on paper or a whiteboard.

# Lesson 83

## porches

**Letters:** | e | o | c | h | p | r | s |  (Rhyming patterns **ore**, **ope**, **ose**)

**Make:** hop   hope   cope   rope   rose   pose   sore   score   shore   chore
porch   porches

**Sort:**

| sore | cope | rose |
|------|------|------|
| core | hope | pose |
| score | rope | |
| chore | | |

**Transfer:** hose        snore        store

## Make Words

- Have children name and hold up letters.
- Tell children how many letters to use to make each word.
- Have children say each word and stretch out some words.
- Give sentences to clarify meaning.
- Give specific instructions on how to change words:
  — Add one letter.
  — Change the first letter.
  — Use the same letters.
- Have children clear their holders before making an unrelated word.
- Have children correct their word once it is made in the pocket chart.
- Give children one minute to figure out the secret word and then give them clues.

## Sort Words

- Put words in pocket chart in the order made.
- Have children say and spell each word.
- Remind them of how each word was changed to spell the new word.
- Select one word from each rhyming set and line up in columns.
- Let children choose the other words that rhyme.
- Have children pronounce the words.

## Transfer Words

- Tell children that they are going to use the rhyming words to spell some new words they might need when they are writing.
- Say the word and a sentence one of your children might write.
- Have children say the word and decide on the beginning letters.
- Write the beginning letters on an index card.
- Take the index card with the beginning letters to the pocket chart and have children say the columns of rhymes and the new word to find the rhyming pattern.
- Write the rhyming pattern on the card to finish the word.
- Have students write the word on paper or a whiteboard.

## teach/cheat

**Letters:** **a** **e** c h t (Rhyming patterns **at**, **ate**, **eat**, **each**)

This lesson has two secret words: **teach** and **cheat**.

**Make:**  at  act  cat  hat  eat  ate  hate  heat  each  cheat  teach

**Sort:**

| eat | cat | each | ate |
|------|------|-------|------|
| heat | at | teach | hate |
| cheat | hat | | |

**Transfer:**  beat    beach    peach

## Make Words

- Have children name and hold up letters.
- Tell children how many letters to use to make each word.
- Have children say each word and stretch out some words.
- Give sentences to clarify meaning.
- Give specific instructions on how to change words:
  — Add one letter.
  — Change the first letter.
  — Use the same letters.
- Have children clear their holders before making an unrelated word.
- Have children correct their word once it is made in the pocket chart.
- Tell children these letters make two secret words. Give children one minute to figure out the secret words and then give them clues.

## Sort Words

- Put words in pocket chart in the order made.
- Have children say and spell each word.
- Remind them of how each word was changed to spell the new word.
- Select one word from each rhyming set and line up in columns.
- Let children choose the other words that rhyme.
- Have children pronounce the words.

## Transfer Words

- Tell children that they are going to use the rhyming words to spell some new words they might need when they are writing.
- Say the word and a sentence one of your children might write.
- Have children say the word and decide on the beginning letters.
- Write the beginning letters on an index card.
- Take the index card with the beginning letters to the pocket chart and have children say the columns of rhymes and the new word to find the rhyming pattern.
- Write the rhyming pattern on the card to finish the word.
- Have students write the word on paper or a whiteboard.

## manager

**Letters:** | a | a | e | g | m | n | r | (Reviews both sounds of **g**)

**Make:** men   man   ran   rag   nag   age   rage   game   name   mean
manage   manager

**Sort:**

| man | rag | age | game |
|-----|-----|------|------|
| ran | nag | rage | name |

**Transfer:** cage   stage   flame

## Make Words

- Have children name and hold up letters.
- Tell children how many letters to use to make each word.
- Have children say each word and stretch out some words.
- Give sentences to clarify meaning.
- Give specific instructions on how to change words:
  — Add one letter.
  — Change the first letter.
  — Use the same letters.
- Have children clear their holders before making an unrelated word.
- Have children correct their word once it is made in the pocket chart.
- Give children one minute to figure out the secret word and then give them clues.

## Sort Words

- Put words in pocket chart in the order made.
- Have children say and spell each word.
- Remind them of how each word was changed to spell the new word.
- Select one word from each rhyming set and line up in columns.
- Let children choose the other words that rhyme.
- Have children pronounce the words.

## Transfer Words

- Tell children that they are going to use the rhyming words to spell some new words they might need when they are writing.
- Say the word and a sentence one of your children might write.
- Have children say the word and decide on the beginning letters.
- Write the beginning letters on an index card.
- Take the index card with the beginning letters to the pocket chart and have children say the columns of rhymes and the new word to find the rhyming pattern.
- Write the rhyming pattern on the card to finish the word.
- Have students write the word on paper or a whiteboard.

# Lesson 86

## target

**Letters:** | a | e | g | r | t | t | (Reviews both sounds of **g**)

**Make:** at art tar rat eat ate age rage rate gate treat target

**Sort:**

| eat | age | gate | at |
|------|------|------|-----|
| treat | rage | ate | rat |
| | | rate | |

**Transfer:** page crate cheat

## Make Words

- Have children name and hold up letters.
- Tell children how many letters to use to make each word.
- Have children say each word and stretch out some words.
- Give sentences to clarify meaning.
- Give specific instructions on how to change words:
  — Add one letter.
  — Change the first letter.
  — Use the same letters.
- Have children clear their holders before making an unrelated word.
- Have children correct their word once it is made in the pocket chart.
- Give children one minute to figure out the secret word and then give them clues.

## Sort Words

- Put words in pocket chart in the order made.
- Have children say and spell each word.
- Remind them of how each word was changed to spell the new word.
- Select one word from each rhyming set and line up in columns.
- Let children choose the other words that rhyme.
- Have children pronounce the words.

## Transfer Words

- Tell children that they are going to use the rhyming words to spell some new words they might need when they are writing.
- Say the word and a sentence one of your children might write.
- Have children say the word and decide on the beginning letters.
- Write the beginning letters on an index card.
- Take the index card with the beginning letters to the pocket chart and have children say the columns of rhymes and the new word to find the rhyming pattern.
- Write the rhyming pattern on the card to finish the word.
- Have students write the word on paper or a whiteboard.

# Lesson 87

## whisper

**Letters:** | e | i | h | p | r | s | w | (Rhyming patterns **is**, **ip**, **ipe**, **ire**)

**Make:** is   his   her   sip   rip   ripe   wipe   wire   hire   ship   whip   whisper

**Sort:**

| his | ship | ripe | wire | sip |
|-----|------|------|------|-----|
| is | whip | wipe | hire | rip |

**Transfer:** fire   strip   stripe

## Make Words

- Have children name and hold up letters.
- Tell children how many letters to use to make each word.
- Have children say each word and stretch out some words.
- Give sentences to clarify meaning.
- Give specific instructions on how to change words:
  — Add one letter.
  — Change the first letter.
  — Use the same letters.
- Have children clear their holders before making an unrelated word.
- Have children correct their word once it is made in the pocket chart.
- Give children one minute to figure out the secret word and then give them clues.

## Sort Words

- Put words in pocket chart in the order made.
- Have children say and spell each word.
- Remind them of how each word was changed to spell the new word.
- Select one word from each rhyming set and line up in columns.
- Let children choose the other words that rhyme.
- Have children pronounce the words.

## Transfer Words

- Tell children that they are going to use the rhyming words to spell some new words they might need when they are writing.
- Say the word and a sentence one of your children might write.
- Have children say the word and decide on the beginning letters.
- Write the beginning letters on an index card.
- Take the index card with the beginning letters to the pocket chart and have children say the columns of rhymes and the new word to find the rhyming pattern.
- Write the rhyming pattern on the card to finish the word.
- Have students write the word on paper or a whiteboard.

# Lesson 88

## drives

**Letters:** | e | i | d | r | s | v | (Rhyming patterns **ed**, **ide**, **ive**, **ine**)

**Make:** is Ed red rid ride side rise dive dives diver drive drives

**Sort:**

| | | | |
|---|---|---|---|
| side | Ed | drive | dives |
| ride | red | dive | drives |

**Transfer:** five      bride      slide

## Make Words

- Have children name and hold up letters.
- Tell children how many letters to use to make each word.
- Have children say each word and stretch out some words.
- Give sentences to clarify meaning.
- Give specific instructions on how to change words:
  — Add one letter.
  — Change the first letter.
  — Use the same letters.
- Have children clear their holders before making an unrelated word.
- Make sure children use a capital **E** when spelling the name **Ed**.
- Have children correct their word once it is made in the pocket chart.
- Give children one minute to figure out the secret word and then give them clues.

## Sort Words

- Put words in pocket chart in the order made.
- Have children say and spell each word.
- Remind them of how each word was changed to spell the new word.
- Select one word from each rhyming set and line up in columns.
- Let children choose the other words that rhyme.
- Have children pronounce the words.

## Transfer Words

- Tell children that they are going to use the rhyming words to spell some new words they might need when they are writing.
- Say the word and a sentence one of your children might write.
- Have children say the word and decide on the beginning letters.
- Write the beginning letters on an index card.
- Take the index card with the beginning letters to the pocket chart and have children say the columns of rhymes and the new word to find the rhyming pattern.
- Write the rhyming pattern on the card to finish the word.
- Have students write the word on paper or a whiteboard.

# Lesson 89

## spelling

**Letters:** | e | i | g | l | l | n | p | s | (Rhyming patterns **ill** and **ell** are introduced.)

**Make:** in   pin   pine   line   slip   pill   gill   sill   sell   spell   spill   spelling

**Sort:**

| in | gill | spell | line |
|----|------|-------|------|
| pin | pill | sell | pine |
| | spill | | |
| | sill | | |

**Transfer:** yell   shell   chill

## Make Words

- Have children name and hold up letters.
- Tell children how many letters to use to make each word.
- Have children say each word and stretch out some words.
- Give sentences to clarify meaning.
- Give specific instructions on how to change words:
  — Add one letter.
  — Change the first letter.
  — Use the same letters.
- Have children clear their holders before making an unrelated word.
- Have children correct their word once it is made in the pocket chart.
- Give children one minute to figure out the secret word and then give them clues.

## Sort Words

- Put words in pocket chart in the order made.
- Have children say and spell each word.
- Remind them of how each word was changed to spell the new word.
- Select one word from each rhyming set and line up in columns.
- Let children choose the other words that rhyme.
- Have children pronounce the words.

## Transfer Words

- Tell children that they are going to use the rhyming words to spell some new words they might need when they are writing.
- Say the word and a sentence one of your children might write.
- Have children say the word and decide on the beginning letters.
- Write the beginning letters on an index card.
- Take the index card with the beginning letters to the pocket chart and have children say the columns of rhymes and the new word to find the rhyming pattern.
- Write the rhyming pattern on the card to finish the word.
- Have students write the word on paper or a whiteboard.

# Lesson 90

## softball

**Letters:** | a | o | b | f | l | l | s | t |  (Rhyming pattern **all** is introduced.)

**Make:** all  ball  tall  fall  boat  soft  loft  fast  last  blast  float  softball

**Sort:**

| all | last | loft | boat |
|------|-------|------|-------|
| tall | blast | soft | float |
| ball | fast | | |
| fall | | | |

**Transfer:** mall  cast  small

## Make Words

- Have children name and hold up letters.
- Tell children how many letters to use to make each word.
- Have children say each word and stretch out some words.
- Give sentences to clarify meaning.
- Give specific instructions on how to change words:
  — Add one letter.
  — Change the first letter.
  — Use the same letters.
- Have children clear their holders before making an unrelated word.
- Have children correct their word once it is made in the pocket chart.
- Give children one minute to figure out the secret word and then give them clues.

## Sort Words

- Put words in pocket chart in the order made.
- Have children say and spell each word.
- Remind them of how each word was changed to spell the new word.
- Select one word from each rhyming set and line up in columns.
- Let children choose the other words that rhyme.
- Have children pronounce the words.

## Transfer Words

- Tell children that they are going to use the rhyming words to spell some new words they might need when they are writing.
- Say the word and a sentence one of your children might write.
- Have children say the word and decide on the beginning letters.
- Write the beginning letters on an index card.
- Take the index card with the beginning letters to the pocket chart and have children say the columns of rhymes and the new word to find the rhyming pattern.
- Write the rhyming pattern on the card to finish the word.
- Have students write the word on paper or a whiteboard.

# Assessnment Lessons 81-90

Write these words in columns and have your children chorally pronounce and spell them. Have them notice that each column of words has the same letters from the vowel to the end of the words and that the words in the column rhyme.

| | | |
|---|---|---|
| **all** | **Bill** | **ride** |
| **call** | **will** | **side** |
| **ball** | **hill** | **slide** |

Have the children number a sheet of paper from 1 to 5. Say a word and put it in a sentence. Ask your students to stretch out each word to hear the beginning letters and then decide which words it rhymes with to finish spelling the word:

| | | | | |
|---|---|---|---|---|
| **tall** | **glide** | **spill** | **chill** | **glide** |

Record their responses on your record sheet. If students did not use the correct pattern or beginning letters, record what they did use and analyze their errors.

Child's Name _____

| Word | Beginning Letters | Rhyming Pattern |
|---|---|---|
| **After Lesson 50** | | |
| mop | m | op |
| tin | t | in |
| flat | fl | at |
| chin | ch | in |
| shop | sh | op |
| **After Lesson 60** | | |
| nut | n | ut |
| jam | j | am |
| slam | sl | am |
| cheat | ch | eat |
| treat | tr | eat |
| **After Lesson 70** | | |
| stay | st | ay |
| dry | dr | y |
| brain | br | ain |
| gray | gr | ay |
| chain | ch | ain |

| Word | Beginning Letters | Rhyming Pattern |
|---|---|---|
| **After Lesson 80** | | |
| track | tr | ack |
| bright | br | ight |
| snack | sn | ack |
| shake | sh | ake |
| fight | f | ight |
| **After Lesson 90** | | |
| tall | t | all |
| bride | br | ide |
| spill | sp | ill |
| chill | ch | ill |
| glide | gl | ide |
| | | |
| | | |
| | | |
| | | |
| | | |

# Lessons 91-100

In these lessons, students learn to decode and spell words with **oo**, **ow**, **ou**, **oy**, **oi**, **ew**, and **aw**.

## Lesson 91

### bookcase

**Letters:**  a, e, o, o, b, c, k, s   (The vowel pair **oo** is introduced.)

**Words to Make:**  so   Bo   boo   book   cook   case   cake   bake   back   sack   sock   bookcase

## Part One • Making Words

Have the children arrange their letters in front of their holders to match the pocket-chart letters, with the vowel first and the other letters in alphabetical order.

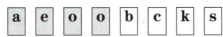

Ask the children to hold up and name each letter and then begin making words.

**so**   "The first word we are going to spell is **so**. I was **so** hungry, I ate two sandwiches. Everyone say **so**."

Choose a child who has **so** spelled correctly to spell **so** with the pocket-chart letters. Have the class chorally spell **so** and fix their word if **so** is not correct.

**Bo**   Change the first letter to spell the name, **Bo**. Do you know anyone named **Bo**? Everyone say **Bo**."

**boo**   "Add 1 letter to spell **boo**. The children scared everyone when they yelled **boo**. Everyone say **boo**."

Let a child who has **boo** spelled correctly spell **boo** with the pocket-chart letters.

**book**   "Add 1 letter to spell **book**. What is your favorite **book**? Everyone say **book**."

Continue the lesson, giving children explicit instruction about which letters to remove and where to add letters. Put each word in a sentence and have children say each word before making it. Have them "stretch" some words to provide practice for children who are still learning to segment words. Let a child who has spelled the word correctly come to the front of the room and make that word with the pocket-chart letters. Choose your struggling readers when the word is an easy word and choose your advanced readers for harder words. Have the children chorally spell each word after it is made in the pocket chart and fix their word to match.

| | |
|---|---|
| **cook** | "Change the first letter to spell **cook**. Do you like to **cook**? Everyone say **cook**." |
| **case** | "Use 4 letters to spell **case**. Put your glasses in their **case**. Everyone say **case**." |
| **cake** | "Change 1 letter to spell **cake**. I love chocolate **cake**. Everyone say **cake**." |
| **bake** | "Change a letter to spell **bake**. I like to **bake** cookies. Everyone say **bake**." |
| **back** | "Use 4 letters to spell **back**. Give yourself a pat on the **back**. Everyone say **back**." |
| **sack** | "Change the first letter to spell **sack**. A **sack** is another name for a bag. Everyone say **sack**." |
| **sock** | "Change the vowel to spell **sock**. I have a hole in my **sock**. Everyone say **sock**." |
| **bookcase** | **(secret word)** "You can make our secret word if you combine 2 words we already made. Make the secret word in your holder and signal me if you think you have figured it out." |

If no one makes the secret word in one minute, give them clues.

End the making words part of the lesson by having **bookcase** spelled in the pocket chart and letting everyone hold up their holders to show you **bookcase** made in their holders. Have them close the holders and turn their attention to the pocket chart.

# Part Two • Sorting Words (Sort for patterns o, ook, ake, ack)

Using the index cards with the words, place them in the pocket chart and have the children pronounce them. Remind the children of what they changed to make each word.

"First we used 2 letters to spell **so**, s-o."

"We changed the **s** to a capital **B** to spell the name **Bo**, B-o."

"We added another **o** to spell **boo**, boo."

"We added the **k** to spell **book**, book."

"We changed the **b** to a **c** to spell **cook**, c-o-o-k."

"We used 4 letters to spell **case**, c-a-s-e."

"We changed 1 letter to spell **cake**, c-a-k-e."

"We changed the **c** to a **b** to spell **bake**, b-a-k-e."

"We used 4 letters to spell **back, b-a-c-k**."

"We changed the **b** to an **s** to spell **sack, s-a-c-k**."

"We changed the vowel to an **o** to spell **sock, s-o-c-k**."

"We combined the words **book** and **case** to spell the secret word, **bookcase, b-o-o-k-c-a-s-e**."

"Now we need to sort out the rhymes. I will take one of each set and you can come and help me find the others."

Arrange one of each set of rhyming words to begin three columns.

| | | | |
|---|---|---|---|
| **so** | **cook** | **bake** | **back** |

Choose three children and help them choose the rhyming words and line them up in columns. Have the rhyming words pronounced and have children notice that they all rhyme and they all have the same letters from the vowel to the end of the word.

| | | | |
|---|---|---|---|
| **so** | **cook** | **bake** | **back** |
| **Bo** | **book** | **cake** | **sack** |

# Part Three ● Transfer  shook   shake   brook

Have the children take out paper. Tell them that you are going to say a word that someone might be writing. By figuring out the rhyming pattern, they will be able to spell the word.

"The first word we are going to spell is **shook**. Cooper might be writing that his dog **shook** water all over him. Let's all say **shook** and listen for the beginning letters."

Write **sh** on an index card when the children decide that **shook** begins with **sh**. Take the index card to the pocket chart and have the children pronounce **shook** with each set of rhyming words. When they decide that **shook** rhymes with book and cook, write **ook** next to **sh**. Have children write **shook** on their papers.

Repeat this procedure for **shake** and **brook**.

## chowder

**Letters:** | e | o | c | d | h | r | w |  (Rhyming patterns **o, ore, ow, ew**)

**Make:**
do  who  how  cow  chow  chew  crew  drew  core
chore  crowd  chowder

**Sort:**

| do | core | cow | chew |
|------|-------|------|------|
| who | chore | chow | crew |
|  |  | how | drew |

**Transfer:**  stew  plow  flew

## Make Words

- Have children name and hold up letters.
- Tell children how many letters to use to make each word.
- Have children say each word and stretch out some words.
- Give sentences to clarify meaning.
- Give specific instructions on how to change words:
  — Add one letter.
  — Change the first letter.
  — Use the same letters.
- Have children clear their holders before making an unrelated word.
- Have children correct their word once it is made in the pocket chart.
- Give children one minute to figure out the secret word and then give them clues.

## Sort Words

- Put words in pocket chart in the order made.
- Have children say and spell each word.
- Remind them of how each word was changed to spell the new word.
- Select one word from each rhyming set and line up in columns.
- Let children choose the other words that rhyme.
- Have children pronounce the words.

## Transfer Words

- Tell children that they are going to use the rhyming words to spell some new words they might need when they are writing.
- Say the word and a sentence one of your children might write.
- Have children say the word and decide on the beginning letters.
- Write the beginning letters on an index card.
- Take the index card with the beginning letters to the pocket chart and have children say the columns of rhymes and the new word to find the rhyming pattern.
- Write the rhyming pattern on the card to finish the word.
- Have students write the word on paper or a whiteboard.

# Lesson 93

## shower

**Letters:** | e | o | h | r | s | w |  (Rhyming patterns **e**, **ore**, **ose**, **ow**)

**Make:**  we   he   her   she   row   show   sore   rose   hose
horse   shore   shower

**Sort:**

| we | sore | rose | row |
|----|------|------|-----|
| he | shore | hose | show |
| she | | | |

**Transfer:**   more       snow       close

## Make Words

- Have children name and hold up letters.
- Tell children how many letters to use to make each word.
- Have children say each word and stretch out some words.
- Give sentences to clarify meaning.
- Give specific instructions on how to change words:
  — Add one letter.
  — Change the first letter.
  — Use the same letters.
- Have children clear their holders before making an unrelated word.
- Have children correct their word once it is made in the pocket chart.
- Give children one minute to figure out the secret word and then give them clues.

## Sort Words

- Put words in pocket chart in the order made.
- Have children say and spell each word.
- Remind them of how each word was changed to spell the new word.
- Select one word from each rhyming set and line up in columns.
- Let children choose the other words that rhyme.
- Have children pronounce the words.

## Transfer Words

- Tell children that they are going to use the rhyming words to spell some new words they might need when they are writing.
- Say the word and a sentence one of your children might write.
- Have children say the word and decide on the beginning letters.
- Write the beginning letters on an index card.
- Take the index card with the beginning letters to the pocket chart and have children say the columns of rhymes and the new word to find the rhyming pattern.
- Write the rhyming pattern on the card to finish the word.
- Have students write the word on paper or a whiteboard.

# Lesson 94
## pilots

**Letters:** `i` `o` `l` `p` `s` `t`  (The vowel pair **oi** is introduced.)

**Make:**  sit  lit  pit  pot  lot  oil  soil  list  spit  spot  spoil  pilots

**Sort:**

| | | |
|---|---|---|
| sit | oil | pot |
| lit | soil | lot |
| pit | spoil | spot |
| spit | | |

**Transfer:**  trot    boil    broil

## Make Words

- Have children name and hold up letters.
- Tell children how many letters to use to make each word.
- Have children say each word and stretch out some words.
- Give sentences to clarify meaning.
- Give specific instructions on how to change words:
  — Add one letter.
  — Change the first letter.
  — Use the same letters.
- Have children clear their holders before making an unrelated word.
- Have children correct their word once it is made in the pocket chart.
- Give children one minute to figure out the secret word and then give them clues.

## Sort Words

- Put words in pocket chart in the order made.
- Have children say and spell each word.
- Remind them of how each word was changed to spell the new word.
- Select one word from each rhyming set and line up in columns.
- Let children choose the other words that rhyme.
- Have children pronounce the words.

## Transfer Words

- Tell children that they are going to use the rhyming words to spell some new words they might need when they are writing.
- Say the word and a sentence one of your children might write.
- Have children say the word and decide on the beginning letters.
- Write the beginning letters on an index card.
- Take the index card with the beginning letters to the pocket chart and have children say the columns of rhymes and the new word to find the rhyming pattern.
- Write the rhyming pattern on the card to finish the word.
- Have students write the word on paper or a whiteboard.

# Lesson 95

## pillows

**Letters:** | i | o | l | l | p | s | w | (Rhyming patterns **ip, ow, ill, oil**)

**Make:** sip  lip  low  slow  lips  slip  will  pill  soil  spoil  spill  pillows

**Sort:**

| sip | slow | will | soil |
|-----|------|------|------|
| lip | low | spill | spoil |
| | | pill | |

**Transfer:** trip  grill  still

## Make Words

- Have children name and hold up letters.
- Tell children how many letters to use to make each word.
- Have children say each word and stretch out some words.
- Give sentences to clarify meaning.
- Give specific instructions on how to change words:
  — Add one letter.
  — Change the first letter.
  — Use the same letters.
- Have children clear their holders before making an unrelated word.
- Have children correct their word once it is made in the pocket chart.
- Give children one minute to figure out the secret word and then give them clues.

## Sort Words

- Put words in pocket chart in the order made.
- Have children say and spell each word.
- Remind them of how each word was changed to spell the new word.
- Select one word from each rhyming set and line up in columns.
- Let children choose the other words that rhyme.
- Have children pronounce the words.

## Transfer Words

- Tell children that they are going to use the rhyming words to spell some new words they might need when they are writing.
- Say the word and a sentence one of your children might write.
- Have children say the word and decide on the beginning letters.
- Write the beginning letters on an index card.
- Take the index card with the beginning letters to the pocket chart and have children say the columns of rhymes and the new word to find the rhyming pattern.
- Write the rhyming pattern on the card to finish the word.
- Have students write the word on paper or a whiteboard.

# Lesson 96

## crawling

**Letters:** a  i  c  g  l  n  r  w  (Rhyming patterns **ail**, **an**, **aw**, **ain**)

**Make:**  can  ran  raw  law  claw  lawn  nail  rail  rain
grain  crawl  crawling

**Sort:**

| nail | can | claw | rain |
|------|-----|------|------|
| rail | ran | raw  | grain |
|      |     | law  |      |

**Transfer:**  paw  tail  brain

## Make Words

- Have children name and hold up letters.
- Tell children how many letters to use to make each word.
- Have children say each word and stretch out some words.
- Give sentences to clarify meaning.
- Give specific instructions on how to change words:
  — Add one letter.
  — Change the first letter.
  — Use the same letters.
- Have children clear their holders before making an unrelated word.
- Have children correct their word once it is made in the pocket chart.
- Give children one minute to figure out the secret word and then give them clues.

## Sort Words

- Put words in pocket chart in the order made.
- Have children say and spell each word.
- Remind them of how each word was changed to spell the new word.
- Select one word from each rhyming set and line up in columns.
- Let children choose the other words that rhyme.
- Have children pronounce the words.

## Transfer Words

- Tell children that they are going to use the rhyming words to spell some new words they might need when they are writing.
- Say the word and a sentence one of your children might write.
- Have children say the word and decide on the beginning letters.
- Write the beginning letters on an index card.
- Take the index card with the beginning letters to the pocket chart and have children say the columns of rhymes and the new word to find the rhyming pattern.
- Write the rhyming pattern on the card to finish the word.
- Have students write the word on paper or a whiteboard.

# Lesson 97

## snowball

**Letters:**  a  o  b  l  l  n  s  w   (Rhyming patterns **o**, **aw**, **all**, **ow**)

**Make:**   no   so   all   saw   law   low   blow   slow   snow   wall   ball   snowball

**Sort:**

| no | saw | wall | low |
|----|-----|------|-----|
| so | law | ball | blow |
|    |     | all  | snow |
|    |     |      | slow |

**Transfer:**   small       claw       grow

## Make Words

- Have children name and hold up letters.
- Tell children how many letters to use to make each word.
- Have children say each word and stretch out some words.
- Give sentences to clarify meaning.
- Give specific instructions on how to change words:
  — Add one letter.
  — Change the first letter.
  — Use the same letters.
- Have children clear their holders before making an unrelated word.
- Have children correct their word once it is made in the pocket chart.
- Give children one minute to figure out the secret word and then give them clues.

## Sort Words

- Put words in pocket chart in the order made.
- Have children say and spell each word.
- Remind them of how each word was changed to spell the new word.
- Select one word from each rhyming set and line up in columns.
- Let children choose the other words that rhyme.
- Have children pronounce the words.

## Transfer Words

- Tell children that they are going to use the rhyming words to spell some new words they might need when they are writing.
- Say the word and a sentence one of your children might write.
- Have children say the word and decide on the beginning letters.
- Write the beginning letters on an index card.
- Take the index card with the beginning letters to the pocket chart and have children say the columns of rhymes and the new word to find the rhyming pattern.
- Write the rhyming pattern on the card to finish the word.
- Have students write the word on paper or a whiteboard.

# Lesson 98

## shouted

**Letters:** | e | o | u | d | h | s | t |  (The vowel pair **ou** is introduced.)

**Make:** out  hut  hot  Ted  shed  shot  shut  hose  house
south  shout  shouted

**Sort:**

| out | Ted | hot | hut |
|-----|-----|-----|-----|
| shout | shed | shot | shut |

**Transfer:** scout   trout   Fred

## Make Words

- Have children name and hold up letters.
- Tell children how many letters to use to make each word.
- Have children say each word and stretch out some words.
- Give sentences to clarify meaning.
- Give specific instructions on how to change words:
  — Add one letter.
  — Change the first letter.
  — Use the same letters.
- Have children clear their holders before making an unrelated word.
- Be sure children use a capital letter when spelling the name **Ted**.
- Have children correct their word once it is made in the pocket chart.
- Give children one minute to figure out the secret word and then give them clues.

## Sort Words

- Put words in pocket chart in the order made.
- Have children say and spell each word.
- Remind them of how each word was changed to spell the new word.
- Select one word from each rhyming set and line up in columns.
- Let children choose the other words that rhyme.
- Have children pronounce the words.

## Transfer Words

- Tell children that they are going to use the rhyming words to spell some new words they might need when they are writing.
- Say the word and a sentence one of your children might write.
- Have children say the word and decide on the beginning letters.
- Write the beginning letters on an index card.
- Take the index card with the beginning letters to the pocket chart and have children say the columns of rhymes and the new word to find the rhyming pattern.
- Write the rhyming pattern on the card to finish the word.
- Have students write the word on paper or a whiteboard.

# Lesson 99

## authors

**Letters:** a o u h r s t (Rhyming patterns **ot, out, our, ut**)

**Make:** hot hat hut out our sour shut shot short shout south authors

**Sort:**

| hot | out | our | hut |
|-----|------|------|------|
| shot | shout | sour | shut |

**Transfer:** pout scout flour

## Make Words

- Have children name and hold up letters.
- Tell children how many letters to use to make each word.
- Have children say each word and stretch out some words.
- Give sentences to clarify meaning.
- Give specific instructions on how to change words:
  — Add one letter.
  — Change the first letter.
  — Use the same letters.
- Have children clear their holders before making an unrelated word.
- Have children correct their word once it is made in the pocket chart.
- Give children one minute to figure out the secret word and then give them clues.

## Sort Words

- Put words in pocket chart in the order made.
- Have children say and spell each word.
- Remind them of how each word was changed to spell the new word.
- Select one word from each rhyming set and line up in columns.
- Let children choose the other words that rhyme.
- Have children pronounce the words.

## Transfer Words

- Tell children that they are going to use the rhyming words to spell some new words they might need when they are writing.
- Say the word and a sentence one of your children might write.
- Have children say the word and decide on the beginning letters.
- Write the beginning letters on an index card.
- Take the index card with the beginning letters to the pocket chart and have children say the columns of rhymes and the new word to find the rhyming pattern.
- Write the rhyming pattern on the card to finish the word.
- Have students write the word on paper or a whiteboard.

# Lesson 100

## destroy

**Letters:** e o d r s t y (The vowel pair **oy** is introduced.)

**Make:** try  dry  Roy  toy  toys  tore  sore  store  story  oyster  destroy

**Sort:**

| try | store | Roy |
|-----|-------|-----|
| dry | tore  | toy |
|     | sore  |     |

**Transfer:** joy  shy  sky

## Make Words

- Have children name and hold up letters.
- Tell children how many letters to use to make each word.
- Have children say each word and stretch out some words.
- Give sentences to clarify meaning.
- Give specific instructions on how to change words:
  — Add one letter.
  — Change the first letter.
  — Use the same letters.
- Have children clear their holders before making an unrelated word.
- Be sure children use a capital **R** when spelling the name **Roy**.
- Have children correct their word once it is made in the pocket chart.
- Give children one minute to figure out the secret word and then give them clues.

## Sort Words

- Put words in pocket chart in the order made.
- Have children say and spell each word.
- Remind them of how each word was changed to spell the new word.
- Select one word from each rhyming set and line up in columns.
- Let children choose the other words that rhyme.
- Have children pronounce the words.

## Transfer Words

- Tell children that they are going to use the rhyming words to spell some new words they might need when they are writing.
- Say the word and a sentence one of your children might write.
- Have children say the word and decide on the beginning letters.
- Write the beginning letters on an index card.
- Take the index card with the beginning letters to the pocket chart and have children say the columns of rhymes and the new word to find the rhyming pattern.
- Write the rhyming pattern on the card to finish the word.
- Have students write the word on paper or a whiteboard.

# Assessment Lessons 91-100

Write these words in columns and have your children chorally pronounce and spell them.

| | | |
|---|---|---|
| not | low | book |
| hot | slow | cook |
| got | snow | took |

Have children write these words, using the rhyming patterns to spell them.

| | | | | |
|---|---|---|---|---|
| shook | grow | spot | crook | flow |

Child's Name _____

| Word | Beginning Letters | Rhyming Pattern |
|---|---|---|
| **After Lesson 50** | | |
| mop | m | op |
| tin | t | in |
| flat | fl | at |
| chin | ch | in |
| shop | sh | op |
| **After Lesson 60** | | |
| nut | n | ut |
| jam | j | am |
| slam | sl | am |
| cheat | ch | eat |
| treat | tr | eat |
| **After Lesson 70** | | |
| stay | st | ay |
| dry | dr | y |
| brain | br | ain |
| gray | gr | ay |
| chain | ch | ain |

| Word | Beginning Letters | Rhyming Pattern |
|---|---|---|
| **After Lesson 80** | | |
| track | tr | ack |
| bright | br | ight |
| snack | sn | ack |
| shake | sh | ake |
| fight | f | ight |
| **After Lesson 90** | | |
| tall | t | all |
| bride | br | ide |
| spill | sp | ill |
| chill | ch | ill |
| glide | gl | ide |
| **After Lesson 100** | | |
| shook | sh | ook |
| grow | gr | ow |
| spot | sp | oy |
| crook | cr | ook |
| flow | fl | ow |

# Reproducible Letters

## Reproducible Consonants

Copy on white card stock, making twice as many letters as you have children.

## Reproducible Vowels

Copy on a different color card stock, making twice as many letters as you have children.

## Reproducible Y

**Y** is sometimes a consonant and sometimes a vowel. Copy on a different color card stock making twice as many letters as you have children.

| b | c | d | f | g | h |
|---|---|---|---|---|---|
| b | c | d | f | g | h |
| b | c | d | f | g | h |
| b | c | d | f | g | h |

| H | G | F | D | C | B |
|---|---|---|---|---|---|
| H | G | F | D | C | B |
| H | G | F | D | C | B |
| H | G | F | D | C | B |

| j | k | l | m | n | p |
|---|---|---|---|---|---|
| j | k | l | m | n | p |
| j | k | l | m | n | p |
| j | k | l | m | n | p |

| P | N | M | L | K | J |
| --- | --- | --- | --- | --- | --- |
| P | N | M | L | K | J |
| P | N | M | L | K | J |
| P | N | M | L | K | J |

| q | r | s | t | v | w |
|---|---|---|---|---|---|
| q | r | s | t | v | w |
| q | r | s | t | v | w |
| q | r | s | t | v | w |

| W | V | T | S | R | Q |
|---|---|---|---|---|---|
| W | V | T | S | R | Q |
| W | V | T | S | R | Q |
| W | V | T | S | R | Q |

| x | z | n | r | s | t |
|---|---|---|---|---|---|
| x | z | n | r | s | t |
| x | z | n | r | s | t |
| x | z | n | r | s | t |

| T | S | R | N | Z | X |
|---|---|---|---|---|---|
| T | S | R | N | Z | X |
| T | S | R | N | Z | X |
| T | S | R | N | Z | X |

| a | e | i | o | u | a |
| e | a | i | o | u | e |
| a | e | i | o | u | i |
| a | e | i | o | u | o |

| A | U | O | I | E | A |
| E | U | O | I | E | A |
| I | U | O | I | E | A |
| O | U | O | I | E | A |

| y | y | y | y | y | y |
| y | y | y | y | y | y |
| y | y | y | y | y | y |
| y | y | y | y | y | y |

| Y | Y | Y | Y | Y | Y |
| Y | Y | Y | Y | Y | Y |
| Y | Y | Y | Y | Y | Y |
| Y | Y | Y | Y | Y | Y |

# Reproducible Record Sheet: Lessons 1–40

Child's Name _____

| Letter | Name | Sound | Word | Segments | | Blends | |
|--------|------|-------|------|----------|--|--------|--|
| **After Lesson 10** | | | | | | | |
| a | | | | sat | | ran | |
| d | | | | band | | last | |
| n | | | | ant | | and | |
| s | | | | rat | | rag | |
| b | | | | past | | trap | |
| t | | | | | | | |
| l | | | | | | | |
| r | | | | | | | |
| p | | | | | | | |
| **After Lesson 20** | | | | | | | |
| c | | | | nut | | tug | |
| f | | | | hunt | | send | |
| g | | | | pet | | pest | |
| h | | | | pin | | trip | |
| m | | | | spot | | mop | |
| **After Lesson 30** | | | | | | | |
| sh | | | | ship | | chip | |
| ch | | | | mash | | cash | |
| th | | | | than | | thin | |
| **After Lesson 40** | | | | | | | |
| j | | | | | | | |
| k | | | | | | | |
| w | | | | | | | |
| a | | | | | | | |
| e | | | | | | | |
| i | | | | | | | |
| o | | | | | | | |
| u | | | | | | | |

# Reproducible Record Sheet: Lessons 41–100

Child's Name _____

| Word | Beginning Letters | Rhyming Pattern |
|------|-------------------|-----------------|
| **After Lesson 50** | | |
| mop | m | op |
| tin | t | in |
| flat | fl | at |
| chin | ch | in |
| shop | sh | op |
| **After Lesson 60** | | |
| nut | n | ut |
| jam | j | am |
| slam | sl | am |
| cheat | ch | eat |
| treat | tr | eat |
| **After Lesson 70** | | |
| stay | st | ay |
| dry | dr | y |
| brain | br | ain |
| gray | gr | ay |
| chain | ch | ain |

| Word | Beginning Letters | Rhyming Pattern |
|------|-------------------|-----------------|
| **After Lesson 80** | | |
| track | tr | ack |
| bright | br | ight |
| snack | sn | ack |
| shake | sh | ake |
| fight | f | ight |
| **After Lesson 90** | | |
| tall | t | all |
| bride | br | ide |
| spill | sp | ill |
| chill | ch | ill |
| glide | gl | ide |
| **After Lesson 100** | | |
| shook | sh | ook |
| grow | gr | ow |
| spot | sp | oy |
| crook | cr | ook |
| flow | fl | ow |

# Reproducible Making Words Take-Home Sheet